THE EVERYDAY
EMBROIDERY BOOK

THE EVERYDAY
EMBROIDERY BOOK

BY

AGNES M. MIALL

DIPLOMA IN DRESSMAKING AND TAILORING
AUTHOR OF
"HOME DRESSMAKING," "MAKING CLOTHES FOR CHILDREN," ETC.

LONDON
SIR ISAAC PITMAN & SONS, LTD.
1936

SIR ISAAC PITMAN & SONS, Ltd.
PITMAN HOUSE, PARKER STREET, KINGSWAY, LONDON, W.C.2
THE PITMAN PRESS, BATH
PITMAN HOUSE, LITTLE COLLINS STREET, MELBOURNE

ASSOCIATED COMPANIES
PITMAN PUBLISHING CORPORATION
2 WEST 45TH STREET, NEW YORK
SIR ISAAC PITMAN & SONS (CANADA), Ltd.
(INCORPORATING THE COMMERCIAL TEXT BOOK COMPANY)
PITMAN HOUSE, 381–383 CHURCH STREET, TORONTO

PREFACE

THIS book is not intended as a manual for the serious student of fancy needlework. It is written rather as a simple and comprehensive guide for the ordinary woman who finds embroidery the most attractive of hobbies. For this reason the stitches and methods described are, in almost all cases, those which give quick results. Women are such busy people nowadays!

I have tried also, in some of the later chapters, to cater briefly for the home embroideress who travels a little now and then and takes a mild interest in the stitchery of other times and other nations. But anything like a general history of embroidery is quite outside the scope of a homely book like this.

The many photographs will, I hope, be of as much help and interest as the letterpress. Here I am glad to acknowledge, with very grateful thanks, the kindness of Dr. Mary Blair in allowing me to photograph for this book her delightful tapestry chair cover (Fig. 74), and of Mr. Ernest Tidbury, who lent me the interesting Spider's Web embroidery, part of which is shown in Fig. 94.

A. M. M.

CONTENTS

ILLUSTRATIONS

ix

THE EVERYDAY EMBROIDERY BOOK

CHAPTER I

PRELIMINARIES

"AND which is your favourite kind of embroidery?" I asked the guest at the boarding-house who spent all her evenings making something pretty.

"Oh, I haven't a favourite kind," she answered at once. "I don't specialize in anything. I just like to work things for the house or clothes or presents and do anything that takes my fancy. Nearly every time it is something different."

That is the kind of home embroideress (there are so very many like her) for whom I am writing this book—the woman who finds embroidery a fascinating hobby and a cheap way of having lovely things she could never afford to buy—not the teacher who must be expert in every kind of work and every stitch, nor the enthusiast who is only interested in doing cross-stitch or cut-work or quilting and doing that one thing superbly.

The majority of women want to embroider nicely, but not with professional expertness. They want to range about as they please among a dozen fascinating kinds of work and know the stitches for these, but not all the stitches that were ever invented. They want embroidery which is beautiful but does not take too long to do, because leisure is limited. It must be easy without being boringly elementary, and something for which they have an everyday use when it is finished.

"Everyday" is the word exactly, isn't it? This is intended to be an everyday embroidery book for everyday needlewomen and I hope that it will become an everyday friend and help.

1

There are home sewers who do wonders in dressmaking and items for the house, but perhaps consider "just making a bit of stuff pretty" rather a waste of time. If you are one of these folk, do think again. Admittedly, we can do without embroidery, whereas we cannot do without curtains and dresses. But you will find that the two types do not clash at all, even from the point of view of time; for there are so many fireside and garden occasions when something to embroider is just what fingers need to keep them from fidgeting, whereas it would not be at all possible, in these informal circumstances, to get out a sewing machine and paper patterns!

Creating beauty has a special thrill of its own and so the world will never be short, I think, of its home embroideresses, who bring colour, design and delicate stitchery to the embellishing of everyday articles.

Tools for Home Embroidery

I will not use the word "equipment," because this gives much too elaborate an idea of what you will need. Of all forms of needlework, simple embroidery depends most on the worker and least on the outfit. The tools needed are therefore very few and simple.

Perhaps the most important item is a pair of fine, sharp, small scissors of the type sold especially for fancy needlework and called embroidery scissors. These are much smaller and more delicate than ordinary sewing scissors; $3\frac{1}{2}$ to 4 inches long is a good size for them. When buying them, see that they have really fine points, are rustless, and preferably made in England of good Sheffield steel.

Although, no doubt, you already have ordinary scissors and cutting-out shears in your work-box, and will use these for the plain sewing parts of embroidered articles, you will find that for snipping your embroidery thread, trimming round scallops, cutting away in cut-work and so on, only the small embroidery scissors are really satisfactory.

It pays to take care of embroidery scissors. Never use them for ordinary coarse sewing purposes, for cutting string or (yes, I have seen it!) for trimming your nails! Keep them for embroidery only and have the blades sharpened when necessary, as, if blunted, they will fray your embroidering thread and cut edges. As the fine points easily blunt in contact with other things in your work-box, it is a good plan to push them, when not in use, into a large medicine-bottle cork.

Needles are the next item on the list. As most kinds cost only twopence a packet and a packet lasts a long time, there is no financial need to try and make one kind do for everything—a system that gives indifferent results! You can well afford to have a packet of each sort needed and always to use the right one for the particular job you are doing.

The short list suggested below will keep you well stocked and give you just the right needle for every kind of embroidery described in this book.

Crewel needles (with large, long eyes to take a thick thread easily). These are for general embroidery use. A packet of mixed sizes from 3 to 7 gives a good assortment.

Wool needles have eyes specially adapted to taking wool and, as wool embroidery is generally only on loosely woven materials which are easily penetrated, blunt points. Use them for the wool embroideries described in Chapter X; also for cross-stitch and tapestry worked in wool, and for wool darning on net.

Rug needles are a much larger and blunter version of wool needles, with a truly enormous eye that will take rug or 8-ply wool. They cost about a penny each, and one will be enough. They have just a few embroidery uses—for instance, when making cut-work bars, to save pricking the fingers; and for bringing through the laid thread at the beginning and end of each thread in rug wool couching.

Millinery straws are sewing needles, fine but extra long, used in hat-making and (in dressmaking) for tacking. They are very convenient for thin quilting done with sewing silk or a strand or two of stranded cotton, as their length enables several stitches to be taken at once.

Punch needles (Fig. 41) are the giants of the embroidery world —so immense that an ordinary thread must be tied into them to keep it in place. Buy just one or two—about two are contained in a twopenny packet—and keep them for punchwork and lace stitch, for which they will make the required big holes.

A stiletto (Fig. 39) is essential for piercing the eyelets in *broderie anglaise*. It is like a miniature dagger set into a handle and costs about sixpence from a fancy needlework shop. Or an excellent, slightly more expensive kind is sometimes obtainable which has a point (one round and one oval) at each end, each of these sliding into the central handle, like a pencil case, when not in use.

If your stiletto is the ordinary kind with an unprotected point, cork this when not in use, as described for embroidery scissors.

A hoop frame is a great help for holding certain types of embroidery which are best worked with the stuff well stretched. This frame is quite cheap and consists of two wooden hoops, one fitting exactly inside the other, with a screw arrangement to ensure tightness. The work is stretched over the inner hoop, the outer one is pushed down over it so that the stuff is held between the two, and the screw is adjusted to keep it taut and prevent any slipping.

Large frames mounted on supports which stand on the table are sold for elaborate professional work, but these are not cheap, nor is it very easy to get the work properly stretched in such a frame. These frames are not needed for any of the embroidery described in this book and are seldom used by the everyday home embroideress.

You will possess already the ordinary sewing tools such as a thimble (take care this is not worn rough, or it will fray your threads), a tape measure and plenty of pins. Steel pins are better than brass ones. For fastening down large appliqués, which are a little difficult to get perfectly flat, a packet of the tiny pins called lillikins is very useful.

YOUR MATERIALS AND EMBROIDERY THREADS

You are neither a professional earning her living by embroidery nor a teacher who must show her pupils the ideal way of doing it. Therefore, you are quite free to use the materials and threads that best suit the work and the use you will put it to when finished, and you need not feel bound to observe what may be called the ritual that surrounds more professional embroidery.

For instance, it is a pity to adopt the idea that linen is the only possible fancywork material, because this fabric, though it wears so wonderfully and embroiders well, is not suitable for all the things you want to make and use. Also the good qualities of linen are rather expensive.

Naturally, if you are setting out to do a beautiful piece of work that is to be an heirloom or has some very special purpose, you will feel that only the best material is good enough for all the work you are going to lavish on it. But in nine cases out of ten you merely want to make some pretty, useful thing which is quite quickly embroidered and will wear out fairly soon.

There is no need, then, to be tied to linen. Other materials, such as a good casement cloth, glass-towelling, house-flannel, madapolam, crash, organdie, felt and various inexpensive silks, may be much more suitable. And remember that a pleasant but thin material, such as sateen, may be successfully embroidered if it is backed with a cotton lining and the work done through both fabrics.

Felt is best backed in the same way with a loose-weave cotton stuff; otherwise, not being woven, but only matted together, it tends to pull out of shape.

Another piece of ritual you should often ignore is the (English only) idea that the natural or beige shade of a fabric is the ideal background for embroidery. Except in a few cases, this is not true. White is a far brighter and cleaner background, and a clear, definite colour is often most successful, especially when embroidered all in white or with black mingled with the embroidering colours.

DO NOT BE AFRAID OF COLOUR. It is at least half the charm of most simple embroideries, as you will see by looking at any kind of peasant work, with its clean, vivid hues and liberal use of black to throw them up. The simpler the type of embroidery or the less your skill in doing it, the more you must rely on a definite and brave colour scheme.

This applies, of course, to threads as well as to backgrounds and appliqués. Modern embroidery threads, whether of cotton, linen, wool or silk, are made in an infinite number of shades, so that there is no difficulty in choosing just the right ones for any particular job. Hints as to the best *type* of thread to use are given under each kind of embroidery in the succeeding chapters.

SOME WORKING HINTS

You will not do your best work unless the light is good. High, reflected lights, unless very well arranged and of good strength, are not as favourable to beautiful work as a concentrated low light, such as a reading lamp, close at hand—preferably on the left side or a little behind the worker.

There are so many kinds of interesting embroidery to choose from that you should avoid doing any type which tries your eyes even when the light is good. This is often a question of the kind of eyesight. If you are short-sighted, you will like and do well detailed work or that with little colour contrast, such as fine cross-stitch and all-white embroideries. If you are long-sighted, these may make your eyes ache, but you will glory in large, splashy jobs —say bold pieces of appliqué, tufting or Italian quilting.

Daintiness and perfect cleanliness are all-important in embroidery. Always wash your hands before starting work, even if they look quite clean. When doing a large embroidery job, roll up the part already done and tack a little tissue paper over it. If you are wearing a dark or non-washable frock, slip over it a clean apron or overall, so that the work will not rub against the dark dress.

Fig. 1 shows a convenient apron with big pockets, easily made at home from a yard of 14-in. Russian crash. Finish one short

FIG. 1. This home-made embroidery apron has capacious pockets
for your work and your tools

edge with a bright binding. Fold this edge upwards to form a pocket about 12 in. deep, seam up the sides and bind the sides and bottom of the apron. Curve and bind the waist, adding strings to tie at the back. Stitch down the centre of the pocket to divide it into two, one for your work and the other for scissors and other tools. Fix a tiny elastic strap across the centre pocket top for your thimble, and just below, if liked, black and white cotton suspended on ribbons.

When work is over for the time being, wrap your embroidery carefully in tissue paper or pop it into your apron or a white washing bag kept for the purpose—do not let it rub up against other things loose in a crowded work-box.

Discard a needle as soon as it becomes bent or blunted. Discard a thread if it becomes roughened, frayed or split when only half used. These may sound extravagant hints, but both needles and thread cost very little—too little to allow them to spoil your beautiful work. Remember that embroidery, whether simple or more elaborate, owes much of its perfection to attention to details.

CHAPTER II

YOUR DESIGN—TRANSFERS

TRANSFERS are to embroidery what paper patterns are to home dressmaking—simply invaluable. Modern transfers are so good and so varied that the home embroideress need seldom want for excellent and attractive designs for any type of fancy stitchery.

Of course, if you have a natural talent for drawing and plenty of leisure, you may like to embark on the fascinating business of drawing your own designs and transferring them to the material by means of carbon paper. But for one person who has the skill and the time to do this, there are a hundred who will infinitely prefer the beauty and ease of bought transfers, which only need to be ironed off on to the chosen fabric. And the hundred are quite right, for without very special talent *and* a long art training they could never hope to evolve for themselves designs half as artistic as those they can buy for a few pence.

When choosing a transfer, you must first decide on the type of embroidery you intend doing in order to have the right design for it. A few transfers serve equally well for two or three kinds of stitchery, but most of them are emphatically not interchangeable and are intended only for a particular class of work.

The majority of transfers are printed only in blue, which is the most generally useful colour, as it irons off well on white and all light and medium shades except blue, mauve, blue-green or yellow-brown. Some transfers are in yellow for use on blue, mauve, black and dark shades, and a few are obtainable in either yellow or blue.

In the last case, supposing that either of these colours marks equally well on your stuff, choose blue, as it is much less trying to the eyes, especially by artificial light.

Correct ironing off of a transfer is important, so that you get a clear outline, neither heavy nor faint and blurred. This is a perfectly easy matter if a few simple hints are borne in mind.

A smooth, padded surface, such as your ironing board, is essential, as any bumps or depressions will prevent the outlines from marking properly. On this surface place the material. It should be right side uppermost, except in the case of firm, transparent materials such as organdie or when ironing off a smocking transfer (see page 147). For these lay the material right side downwards.

Not all transfers require the same amount of heat to "take," this varying with the material and also with the colour of the transfer. For instance, usually a hotter iron is required for designs printed in blue than for those in yellow. Because of these individual variations, it is always best to cut off from the transfer any odd bit not required for the embroidery (such as the transfer number or the maker's name) and test this first on an oddment of the same material, to note the right heat of the iron.

You can judge of this by the results. Too cool an iron gives too faint an impression or even none at all. On the other hand, too much heat will produce an outline which is over-heavy and thick or blurred—this last may also be caused by the transfer having shifted under the iron.

A clear, firm outline, looking the same all over, is what you must aim at. Uneven marking may mean that the surface beneath the material is not smooth or that the iron has cooled during the stamping. This may happen if the transfer is a large one, or if a whole set, such as thirteen lunch mats, is being marked at once.

Having made your test, lay the transfer, face downwards, over the material in the correct position. (The face of the transfer is its darker, shiny side.) Be careful that the design (not the edges of the paper on which it is printed) is well placed, exactly in the centre, if it is to be a centre design, or truly parallel with the hem or straight edge in the case of a border.

Sometimes, particularly in dress embroidery, the design may have to go over a seam, as when embroidering all round the hem of a child's frock. In this case stitch the seam and press it as flat as possible before stretching the transfer right across it. It may mark a little unevenly just across the seam if this is bumpy.

Pin the transfer to the material with enough pins to keep the two layers from shifting under the iron; but place the pins as far as possible from the actual design, so that the iron need not pass over them.

Now press with an iron of the correct heat all over the uppermost (wrong) side of the transfer. Use a thumping, not a gliding movement, putting the iron down firmly and lifting it off before stamping it down again in another spot. After doing one corner, unpin and lift just a scrap of the transfer and note what sort of outline you are getting.

Take care the iron goes well over the points and corners of the design. It is easy to press beautifully in the centre, but to give the extremities so little stamping that the design fades out at these points.

As I have said, yellow designs mostly require less heat than blue ones, so a good plan with these is either to use a cooler iron or to press over two thicknesses of newspaper, which will absorb some of the heat before it reaches the transfer.

Smooth materials take the design better than rough ones, and the thinner the material, generally speaking, the less heat will be needed. Stamp very thin fabrics (especially organdie, which curls up annoyingly under quite ordinary heat) with a rather cool iron, interposing a double or a single layer of tissue paper between the iron and the transfer.

When the ironing off is complete and the used transfer unpinned from the material, keep the transfer, at any rate for a time. It will not stamp off again, of course, but you can cut it up and use the pieces as patterns for cutting appliqués, if you are doing this type of work. Or if you want to use the same design again you can trace it through carbon paper in the way described for original designs on page 20.

Keep transfers, whether old, or new ones awaiting use, in

envelopes, as they soon get crumpled and spoilt if loose in your work-box.

Sometimes, if you have not been careful in looking over your transfer and cutting away any unwanted sprays, numbers, etc.,

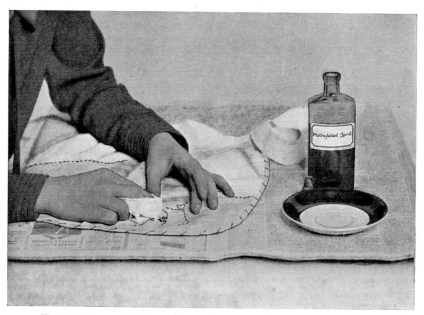

Fig. 2. Unwanted transfer markings can often be removed with methylated spirit

before pinning it down, you may find your design marred by lines which you do not want to embroider. It is not easy to remove transfer stamping, but on many materials it can be done without spoiling or soiling the surface.

It is best to stamp an odd bit of transfer on a scrap of the same stuff and experiment with that first. Washable materials may be well dabbed with a soapy lather and then rinsed in the same way. If this does not take them out, or if the material will not stand soap and water, rub the unwanted markings with either methylated spirit (as in Fig. 2) or benzine. It depends on the composition of the transfer which works best. More than one application may be needed.

Invaluable though transfers are, there are a few materials for which they should not be used. On flimsy transparent stuffs, such as ninon or georgette, the outline made is too heavy. In such cases, tack the transfer, right side uppermost against the wrong side of the material, through which it will show clearly. Embroider through both stuff and transfer, afterwards tearing the latter away.

Pile, crêpe and very rough-surfaced fabrics also fail to retain a transfer, while the iron, in addition, flattens pile materials. Such materials are not usually very suitable for embroidery; but if it is undertaken on them, tack the transfer over the right side of the material, work through transfer and stuff and then tear away the paper as described above.

For the best method of transferring a design of your own on to material, see the next chapter.

Chapter III

YOUR DESIGN—BUILT-UP PATTERNS

HOWEVER much you rightly rely on transfers for most of your home embroidery, there are a few occasions when they do not quite meet the case and you will find that it is better to evolve a simple spray or pattern of your own.

No, I do not mean anything nearly as elaborate as drawing out original designs to scale on paper. As I suggested in Chapter II, very few home fancyworkers have the skill and the patience to do this. But suppose you merely want a simple but pretty border to finish off a sewing job or one small motif that can hardly be dignified by the name of a design?

As a rule, there is little choice of transfers for these very simple things. Again, you may be in a hurry and the shops are closed or you live in the country a long way from any embroidery shop at all! Isn't it convenient then—not to say interesting—to know how to build up an easy border or motif that is just what you want?

This kind of designing is not in the least difficult, because it really is a gradual building up or combining of very simple stitches and shapes into something charmingly decorative. There is no drawing to bother with, beyond ruling a line or two or pencilling round something circular for guidance. Given some such elementary foundation, you simply make up the pattern or motif as you go along. You will find that the first kind of stitch, once in place, suggests a second and that leads to a third. For a simple built-up design it is usually best not to use more than three different stitches.

As a rule, the simpler the stitch the better it combines with others to form patterns. Stitches I have found specially helpful in building-up are stroke-stitch, lazy-daisy, French knots (these three are described and illustrated in Chapter IV), buttonhole

14

stitch (Chapter V), running-stitch (Chapter VI), fly-stitch (Chapter IX), ladder-stitch (Chapter XI), cross-stitch (Chapter XIII) and herringbone and feather-stitches (Chapter XIV).

Do not carry out your experimenting on the actual garment or item to be adorned or you may spoil it with various unpickings. Try your idea first on an oddment of stuff, or keep a piece of material for use as a sampler of patterns, so that you can repeat a successful one if the item for which it was originally invented is worn out or given away.

No set rules can be given for building up, because it depends so very much on the inspiration of the moment. You must, of course, begin by deciding on the shape and size of your border or motif; then mark its outlines on the material with tacking, tailor's chalk or faint pencil lines, according to the nature of the stuff. For a border, it is a good plan to rule either a central straight line on each side of which the pattern will be built or two parallel lines inside which it must evolve.

This kind of pattern-making is really great fun! To show how the designs grow, let us take the process of building up those illustrated in this chapter. Always give your patterns names, by the way. It identifies them and also makes you feel much prouder of having invented them!

"*Peeping Through the Fence.*" (Fig. 3.) I started this impressive border, $2\frac{1}{4}$ in. wide when completed, by marking three parallel straight lines each $\frac{1}{2}$ in. apart. Along each outer line I worked blanket-stitch (see page 43) so that the purl or cord of the stitches came along these two outer lines and the two lines of stitchery met on the centre line.

When I had done this I got the idea of a fence, and proceeded to equip it top and bottom with a barbed-wire effect. This was done by working a fly-stitch (page 96) point outwards, over the purl of each blanket-stitch, with single stroke stitches between as if to impale trespassers! The middle line now looked a little bare, but a French knot between every blanket-stitch gave an impression of a head peeping through. And that's all!

You will see that in this border I broke the rule given above and used four different stitches, but the border is rather a wide one and blanket and fly-stitches very similar in character, so that the effect is not fidgety.

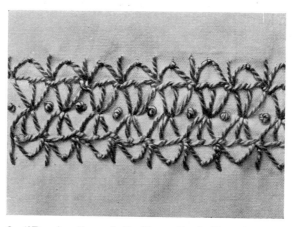

Fig. 3. "Peeping through the Fence," a built-up border using blanket-, fly- and stroke-stitches and French knots

If a two-colour effect is wanted when copying "Peeping through the Fence," make the French knots decidedly darker than the rest.

"*Desert Skyline.*" (Fig. 4.) A poetical name for a very simple border using only two stitches. It is worked above the hem of a runner made of linen glass-towelling checked in inch squares, but could be carried out in plain material by pencilling a horizontal line for the sand and short upright ones for the group of cactus plants.

Work the ground line in running-stitch (page 55). Alternate long and short cacti, working these in one-way feather-stitching (Chapter XIV)—that is, feather-stitch with all "prongs" on one side, instead of on each side alternately. Then work a second line of feather-stitch back to back with the first, but this time with all prongs on the other side and pairing off with the first set.

By making the lines of feather-stitch rather taller, with the prongs straight out instead of slanting upwards, and each prong a little longer than the one above, the design becomes a row of Christmas trees.

FIG. 4. This original border in feather- and running-stitches is aptly named "Desert Skyline"

Work the stitches in a thick matt cotton thread, such as Artello Twist.

Still keeping to straight lines, suppose we evolve a slim upright panel instead of a border, to adorn each end of a linen runner or tray-cloth. We might call this "Excelsior" after the hero of Longfellow's poem who climbed ever higher.

"*Excelsior.*" To copy the design as shown in Fig. 5, at right-angles to the edge mark out a panel $6\frac{3}{4}$ in. high by 1 in. wide on green linen. Starting along the marked outlines and working outwards, so that the panel size is considerably increased, work two lines of white running-stitch, next two of dark green and outside these two of parma violet. The linen edge should be fringed to a depth of $\frac{3}{4}$ in. and the darning wool run down into the fringe at the beginning and end of each line.

To make the long spray of berries inside the panel, work a slightly zigzag vertical line of dark green back-stitches, each $\frac{1}{4}$ in. long, down the centre. At the outward point of each work a single mauve lazy-daisy stitch. Fill each lazy-daisy with a white stroke stitch, and the apparently elaborate decoration is complete.

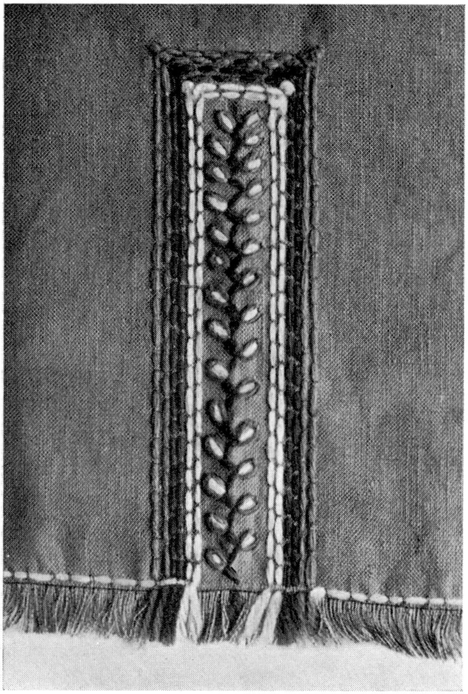

Fig. 5. A striking panel built up on a few simple stitches and called "Excelsior"

Before leaving the subject of patterns based on straight lines, there is another (not illustrated) which uses the diamond. Two narrow lines of the pattern, preferably separated with bar hem-stitching rows (see page 112), makes an attractive colourful border of a formal kind. Here it is.

"*Diamonds are Trumps.*" Work this on crash or some other material on which threads are easily counted. In black, work a row of touching cross-stitches (page 139) to form a continuous line of small diamonds. Leave three blank, fill the next three with orange satin-stitch (page 73), leave the third three blank, fill the fourth trio with green satin-stitch, and so on all along.

Motifs are often prettiest with a circle as a foundation. Circles of various sizes are easily obtained by drawing round copper coins, egg-cups, tea-cups, and so on; while if a heart or diamond shape is wanted, a set of tin sandwich cutters for bridge parties gives these outlines in a handy form.

Motifs are frequently better than borders for corners, collar points, patch pockets and so on.

"Autumn's Harvest" (Fig. 6) shows a built-up motif for a duchesse set that could not well be simpler. Each mat has a machine hem-stitched panel set well inside its lace-trimmed edges. Two rows of alternating running-stitches, the first in scarlet, the second in green, are woven in and out of the hem-stitch. Across one corner only of this on each mat mark two interlaced circles, one large and one small, their sizes varying with that of the mat.

At short intervals all round the circles work groups of six French knots, five grouped round

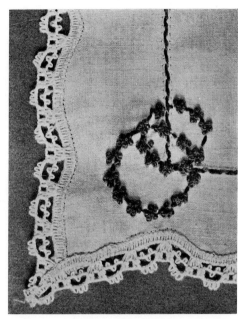

FIG. 6. "Autumn's Harvest" is a simple French knot design based on circles

a central one, using all six strands of scarlet stranded cotton. Between them run the circle outlines in green. Effective, you'll admit!

Again, the *broderie anglaise* spray in Fig. 37, page 70, shows how a graceful design may be based on a circle merely by adding two side curves which it does not take an artist to draw! Graduated circles combined with straight lines give effective patterns for quilting, and very attractive borders or motifs may be built up on triangles.

In fact, if you once get interested, as you can hardly help doing, there is really no end to pattern-making without transfers.

Transferring Your Own Design to the Material

You may be one of the accomplished few who can draw quite elaborate original designs. Or you may want to use a design which is outlined to the full size in a magazine for you to transfer to your stuff.

The easiest plan, in either case, is to buy a sheet of *embroidery* carbon paper (not the typewriter kind) from a fancy needlework shop. The usual colour is black, but one or two other shades are usually obtainable for use on blue or black materials. The use of this carbon is a little laborious but not at all difficult.

First, pin down your material with drawing-pins, which should be taut but not tightly stretched, to a soft wooden surface, such as a drawing-board, pastry board or whitewood kitchen table. Lay your sheet of carbon paper over the part of the material where the design is to come, with the shiny side downwards, i.e. against the material. Lay the drawn-out design over this and hold all three layers together and to the board with drawing-pins. As the latter may mark closely-woven fabrics, place them, if possible, near the edges of the stuff.

Carefully go over the outlines of the design, taking care not to lose their curves and delicacy, with a steel knitting needle, an orange stick, a stiletto or a hard pencil. Experiment first with scraps of stuff, carbon and design paper to see which instrument gives the best outline, as this varies with the fabric and the drawing paper.

When tracing on to delicate or pale materials, take great care not to rest the hand heavily while tracing or to smear it across the paper. If you do so, the carbon may smudge and discolour the fabric; but with a little care and lightness of touch all will be well.

After tracing, unpin the three layers, when the design should be clearly marked on the material.

There are other methods of transferring designs, but they are much more troublesome, so I should recommend you to keep to carbon paper on the (probably) rare occasions when you need to trace a design. It is worth remembering that this plan can also be employed if you want to use a bought transfer a second time. In this case do your tracing from the ironed-off transfer.

CHAPTER IV

OUTLINE EMBROIDERIES

I THINK it is safe to say that outline embroideries are the most popular of all in these days of scanty leisure, because they give a good and colourful effect for the least possible amount of work. The stitches used are the simplest there are, so that even a person with very little knowledge of fancy stitchery can do this kind of embroidery with success.

If you are interested in teaching a child or children to embroider, make a start with outline work, because it is so simple and the job is done before an impatient little girl has time to tire of it. For the same reason, a busy mother who wants touches of handwork on her little people's clothes can add them in outline very rapidly.

The term "outline embroidery" is used to denote any kind of fancy stitchery in which the design is carried out by merely out-lining—not filling in—the various portions. A number of different stitches are used, and numerous different types of designs are available; but a feature always found in outline embroidery is the use of bright coloured working threads and designs which have a very definite form and interest.

Outline embroideries, you see, do not cover the surface or permit of any shading, so they must rely on colour and line. See that the working threads contrast sharply with the background material and with each other and that the design used has a real interest of its own. Flower patterns are not generally so successful, unless they are the daisy type which can be carried out in lazy-daisy stitch (see *B* and *C* in Fig. 7) as the "picture" kind of design, such as the dancing rabbits in Fig. 8 and the breezy seascape in Fig. 10.

As to colour, outline embroidery is one of those types which are definitely successful on natural backgrounds. The neutral tone throws up the brilliant colours that should be used for embroidering

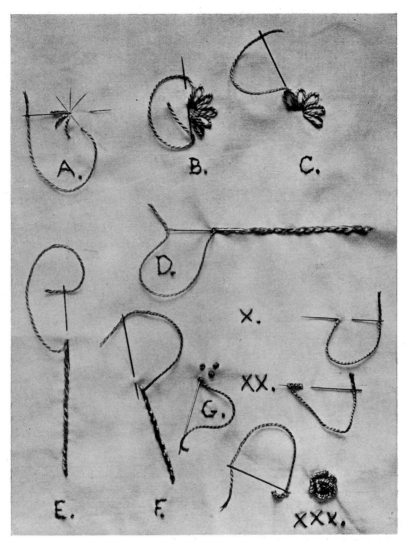

FIG. 7. A useful sampler of outline stitches, showing the working of:
A, stroke-stitch; *B* and *C*, lazy-daisy; *D*, split-stitch; *E*, outline-
stitch; *F*, stem-stitch; *G*, French knots; *X*, *XX* and *XXX*, stages
of bullion-stitch

(see Fig. 8). Another good choice is white material (used for the mat in Fig. 9), while all-white outlining on a brilliant-coloured material, though rather rare, can look extremely well. A touch of black is nearly always an advantage.

Fig. 8. A lively outline design for a child's bib sachet worked in outline and stroke-stitches, with a border of spaced buttonholing

Do not put vivid embroidery, except white or black, on a bright background, as the outline stitches are too thin to show up against such full-toned material.

When choosing a floral outline design, select a concentrated one, like the basket of flowers in Fig. 9. Thin sprays sprawling all over the material look poor and uninteresting when worked only in outline.

There is a large choice of outline stitches and you will not need to use them all in a single piece of work. In fact, designs are often carried out in one stitch only; Fig. 52, page 91, shows an example of this, a spray of tulips and leaves worked in wool entirely in outline-stitch. But, generally speaking, the effect is more varied and interesting if three or four different stitches are used.

For instance, the rabbit design in Fig. 8 combines outline and stroke stitches. For the mat in Fig. 9, running-stitch (Fig. 27, page 55), cross-stitch (Fig. 70), lazy-daisy, French knots and satin-stitch (page 73) are used, while the ships and

FIG. 9. Mat in outline embroidery with cross-stitch border

seagulls in Fig. 10 are carried out in outline stitch and couching (Fig. 15).

All the most popular outline stitches, except the few already given where another illustration number is quoted, are shown clearly in Fig. 7. If you are an absolute beginner at embroidery and start, as you should, with outline work, these various simple stitches which you must learn will give you a splendid foundation for other kinds of fancy work which you may try later on. Practically all of them have many other uses outside outline embroidery.

Here are working descriptions of those shown in Fig. 7. They are identified by the letters of the alphabet embroidered close to each in back-stitch or cross-stitch, both of these being useful outline stitches.

Stroke-stitch or Straight-stitch (Fig. 7, *A*). The simplest stitch in the whole field of embroidery. It is a very quick way of working small star-like flowers indicated on a transfer by straight lines or for tiny leaves of the same sort. Bring the needle up at one end of the line and take it down to the wrong side at the other, at the same time re-inserting it at the end of the next line ready for a second stitch. Pull up the thread so that the stitch lies along the line, being neither slack nor taut enough to pucker the material.

Lazy-daisy, sometimes called Loop-stitch (Fig. 7, *B* and *C*). One of these quick stitches embroiders an entire small leaf or daisy petal—hence it is the lazy or busy person's best friend! It is used for both flowers and leaves in Fig. 9 and for the small leaflets in Fig. 66.

To work the stitch, bring the needle through from the wrong side at the centre end of a flower petal or the stem end of a leaf. Holding down the thread with the left thumb, put the needle back into the stuff where it came out and let it re-emerge to the right side at the outer end of the petal or leaf (*B* in Fig. 7). Still holding down the loop of thread thus formed under the needle, pull the needle right through. Draw up the thread till the loop lies rather loosely on the surface. Hold the loop down at its outer end by now taking a tiny stroke-stitch across it, as at *C* in Fig. 7.

For filled lazy-daisy stitch see page 30.

Split-stitch (*D*, Fig. 7) gives a thin, chain-like outline, rather like chain-stitch (see page 107), but narrower and flatter. The stitch can be used for long outlines, such as those of stems, or for holding down a hem round an item embroidered in outline stitches. Employ it sometimes as a change from outline stitch. It is quickly worked and not as well known as it deserves to be.

Use a rather broad, thick thread. Proceed as for the outline stitch (see below), working upwards or away from you; but instead of keeping the thread to the left of the needle, as for the outline-stitch, pass the needle through it each time, splitting the thread—hence the name, split-stitch.

Outline-stitch (*E*, Fig. 7) is very useful indeed for stems, frame lines round work and outlines generally. It is used almost entirely for working the rabbit design in Fig. 8 and for the seagulls in Fig. 10.

Start at the bottom of the line to be covered and work upwards. Bring the needle through from the wrong side; then from a little higher up the line take a stitch downwards and backwards. While doing this, be sure to keep the thread to the left of, and underneath, the needle, as in the illustration. Pull up the thread. Pick up a second similar stitch from above and work downwards, taking the bottom of this just to the top of the first stitch. Continue similarly upwards.

Stem or Crewel-stitch (*F*, Fig. 7). Work just as for outline-stitch (above) but with these two differences: (1) start each stitch half-way down the previous one, instead of just at the top of it; (2) keep the thread always to the right of and below the needle, instead of to the left of it.

This stitch is used for much the same purposes as the outline-stitch, but it gives a rather thicker outline, so that it is preferable where slightly more weight is wanted. It is not, however, so smooth as outline stitch. In Fig. 7, where the two are side by side (*E* and *F*) the differences can be noted.

French Knots (*G*, Fig. 7). These raised, detached knots are very decorative for flower centres (one for a small flower, a cluster of them for a larger one), to fill spaces in a built-up border (see Fig. 3), for eyes in an animal or human picture design or to form groups of tiny berries, as in Fig. 6. Or complete outlines may be carried out in French knots spaced $\frac{1}{2}$ in. apart, giving an effect very like that of beads.

Some people also like to hold down hems or adorn neck-lines in children's clothes with spaced knots. For hems, such knots have the advantage of being easily cut away without leaving marks if lengthening is needed.

To make French knots, bring the needle through from the wrong side just where the knot is to be. Twist the thread once, twice or three times (according to the size of knot required) round the needle, and while doing this hold down the free part of the thread above the twisted part. Still holding the thread, return the needle to the wrong side as close as possible to where it first emerged, as at *G*, Fig. 7.

Bullion-stitch is a near relation of the French knot. It is a much more imposing version which, instead of being round, forms a long or curved roll. Its three stages of making are shown in Fig. 7 at *X*, *XX* and *XXX* respectively. Perhaps it is hardly an outline stitch, as it more or less covers the surface it is on, but it is convenient to describe it here with the French knot, and it is mostly used on designs which are otherwise in outline.

As *XXX* (Fig. 7) shows, three or four bullion-stitches laid close together, or coiled round each other, make very naturalistic tiny roses—the sort indicated in a transfer by small circles. Some people also make each petal of a small daisy from a long bullion-stitch, giving the flower a French knot centre.

Bring the needle through at one end of the line or space the stitch is to cover. Insert it from the right side at the other end of the line or space and let it emerge again just at the starting point, as at *X*, Fig. 7. The needle should come only half-way through, as shown. Wind the thread tightly round the forepart of the needle from four to ten times, according to the length of stitch wanted, as at *XX*. It is usually easier to wind counter-clockwise, that is, over from right to left and under from left to right.

Holding the windings closely to the needle (*not* the slack thread down to the stuff, as when making French knots), pull the needle through the windings without disarranging them. Hold them as long as possible during pulling, then swing them over to cover the line or space the stitch is to occupy and hold down with a stitch to the wrong side as at *XXX*.

I have described this stitch very fully, because personally I consider it a distinctly tricky one, the knack of which takes a little time to acquire. When well made, it should form a smooth, even roll, as at *XXX*, Fig. 7.

However, if you try it and do not find it easy (some people do!)

here is a simple way out that I have discovered. Make an overcast bar (see page 83) by laying a long stroke-stitch and then overcasting closely over and over it (not into the stuff as well). *Hey presto!* The effect is exactly that of a bullion-stitch. Of course, it takes longer to do, so that it is advisable to use it only in a piece of work where not many such stitches are required.

Bullion-stitch flowers are often combined with drawn-in drawn-thread work (see page 118), and they are shown worked in this way in Fig. 66, page 119.

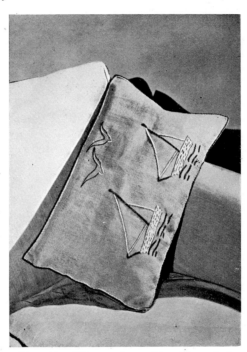

The foregoing stitches, all illustrated in Fig. 7, are the main ones you will need for working outline embroideries. Other stitches often used for this kind of fancy work are cross-stitch (see Fig. 9), back-stitch (see Fig. 27) and couching, in which the cushion in Fig. 10 is mainly carried out. But as these three stitches

FIG. 10. This crash cushion is worked mainly in couching, using chenille for the laid thread

all have more important uses in other forms of embroidery, they are fully described and illustrated in later chapters—couching as an appliqué stitch, back-stitch for use in quilting and cross-stitch under this kind of embroidery in Chapter XIII.

Chain-stitch (Chapter XI) is also an effective outline-stitch when a rather wide and noticeable effect is wanted. Turn to page 101 and notice how handsome it looks in the monogram in Fig. 58.

You will perhaps smile if I mention the value of satin-stitch in outline embroideries—and your smile will be because this is the

most solid-looking of all stitches and least of all an outline one in appearance. The same applies to filled lazy-daisy stitch (Fig. 11).

Actually my suggestion is not as strange as it sounds. As you will see by the various illustrations in this chapter, outline work has an inevitable tendency, despite interesting design and gay colour, to look a little thin. So it is often a good plan to give more "body" and provide a focal point for the eye, by working just a small part of the design in the very solid-looking satin-stitch.

FIG. 11. Working filled lazy-daisy stitch.
Use a double thread for the filling

Do not overdo this, of course. In Fig. 9 only the ribbon tying the basket handle is satin-stitched—but how it does hold the whole design together! Sometimes open lazy-daisy flowers gain greatly if their centres are filled in with a stroke-stitch in wool (Fig. 5) or a silk one worked in double thread, as in Fig. 11. The latter stitch, by the way, is called filled lazy-daisy.

Again, in Fig. 66, page 119, the compact bullion-stitch flowers give enough weight to the very airy lazy-daisy leaves and drawn-in drawn-threadwork lines.

In fact, in outline embroidery, as in most other things, an ounce of cunning is worth a pound of mere painstaking.

CHAPTER V

APPLIQUÉ AND INLAY

A FAVOURITE form of embroidery is appliqué—and no wonder! For if you want to get a bold, handsome and solid effect full of gay colour, without the labour of embroidering your whole design in satin-stitch, appliqué is just the right method.

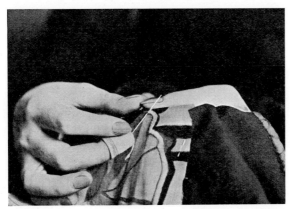

FIG. 12. Applying a cretonne motif to a cushion; working the buttonholed edge

The word itself is the French for "applied," and it is by applying one material over another and holding it down just round its edges that you obtain such an imposing result for so little work.

There are several kinds of appliqué and you will be enthusiastic about each in turn, for all are so striking and colourful.

This kind of embroidery may be used for almost anything, but as it covers large areas rapidly and is distinctly bold in its effects, it is particularly suitable for rather big items, such as cushion covers (Fig. 13), wall panels or pictures (Fig. 14), pram covers, curtains, fire-screens, laundry bags, and so on.

31

Appliqué used to be avoided for items which were being continually washed, such as table linen, owing to its use of much
colour. This point is not so important now that most fabrics are
colour-fast, and appliqué is now quite a favourite for luncheon
table mats, or, when only white and a single colour are used, as in
Fig. 96, it is delightful for tray-cloths and duchesse sets.

Another use of appliqué is for certain very charming dress
embroideries, when it may make a bright spot of colour on a pocket
or delicately adorn underwear. For lingerie, the contrast of the
appliqué with the background is one of material rather than vivid
colour, and it is worked in smaller designs and daintier effects than
for trimming household furnishings.

Of the several kinds of appliqué, suppose we take the easiest
one first.

Cretonne Appliqué

Here there is no building up of a design with piecemeal appliqués.
Instead a great deal of work is saved and a very good effect gained
by cutting out a ready-made design from a patterned material and
holding this down to the background with simple stitches. Often,
but not always, a few details in the design are emphasized by being
worked over in outline stitches.

Fig. 13 gives you a good idea of how effective this kind of
appliqué can be. It shows a water-lily motif cut from cretonne and
applied to a strongly contrasting cushion (different in both colour
and texture), and with the main lines of the design picked out in
chain-stitch.

Cretonne appliqué is so called because it is easier to cut suitable
designs from cretonne than from most fabrics, but other materials
can be—and often are—used. For instance, for small appliqués on
dress items, handkerchiefs, sachets and so on, attractive designs
may often be found on printed dress cottons or floral silks or voiles.

Remember, when choosing a material for your appliqués, that
you need one which has definite sprays of flowers or berries, little
landscape scenes or geometrical patterns which are detached or,
at any rate, can be cut away in a complete form from the rest of

the design. Intertwined or very all-over patterns are seldom suitable.

There are two rather different ways of applying cretonne appliqués. It depends partly on your own preference and partly on the appliqué material which you choose. You will probably find

Fig. 13. The finished cretonne appliqué on the cushion cover.
Its main outlines are chain-stitched

it wise to know both methods and to use whichever seems best for the particular job you are doing.

The margin method is the older of the two. It needs less preparatory work but more finishing, and is the better plan if the appliqué material frays easily or the work is likely to be a long time in hand. The cushion cover was worked by this method, which is shown in progress in Fig. 12.

Begin by cutting out the appliqué only roughly, with good margins or turnings all round it. Lay it in the correct position on the background material, with the wrong side of the appliqué against the right side of the material. Pin it down carefully so that it lies perfectly smooth everywhere. If required, to preserve this smoothness while embroidering, next tack it just inside the actual edges of the design.

Unless the appliqué is a very small one, this tacking is always advisable, as it holds the two layers together with absolute flatness and avoids the use of pins which will probably catch in the embroidery thread.

Fig. 12 shows how the appliqué is then held down to the background by working a close, smooth buttonhole-stitch along the edges of the design, with the purl or corded edge lying exactly along the edge. (For the working of buttonhole-stitch see page 40.) Embroider any details in the interior of the design which you think need to be emphasized in any of the suitable outline stitches given in Chapter IV, or (for a large design) in the bolder chain-stitch (see page 107).

The final step is to take your small, sharp embroidery scissors and carefully cut away the surplus or margin appliqué material outside the buttonhole stitching. Cut as close as possible to the purl edge, so that no appliqué fabric will show outside it, but take great care not to cut into the purl edge itself and into the background material.

The cut-out method is more modern and consequently more popular nowadays. Use it for materials which do not fray readily and when the work will not lie about unfinished for long; also when you have so little appliqué material that you cannot allow margins round the design.

With embroidery scissors cut out the design very carefully and accurately, right along its edges, without any turnings. Lay and pin it on the material as for the margin method, holding it down after pinning by going all round the edges with a running stitch or hemming in matching sewing cotton. Then cover the caught-down edges either with close buttonhole stitching or with couching (for the working of the latter stitch see page 43).

Work any interior details as for the margin method.

Embroidered (or Built-up) Appliqué

While all forms of appliqué are more or less embroidered, this type owes more to fancy stitchery than the others and so earns its right to the name. Here the design is built up piece by piece, each portion being embroidered into place. This is, perhaps, the most decorative kind of appliqué.

At art needlework shops you can buy items ready stamped and

FIG. 14. A picture, carried out in embroidered appliqué on black linen that suggests Spring

with the appliqué pieces, each in its correct colour, already pasted into position. This saves trouble, especially if the design used is a complicated one with many little pieces in it, like the bowl of crocuses and snowdrops shown in Fig. 14. But the paste used for affixing the appliqués stiffens the fabric and often makes the stitchery rather hard work.

On the other hand, as pasted edges do not fray, they can be finished with couching (see page 43) or spaced buttonholing, both of which are much quicker than close buttonhole stitching. Fig. 14 shows these two stitches well balanced and combined, the bowl and crocuses being in spaced buttonholing, with the more delicate snowdrops outlined in the lighter and thinner couching.

Another plan, just as popular as ready-prepared appliqués, is to buy your own background material and an effective appliqué transfer, and to build up the design piece by piece from odd scraps of material in the right colours. Every home needlewoman has an

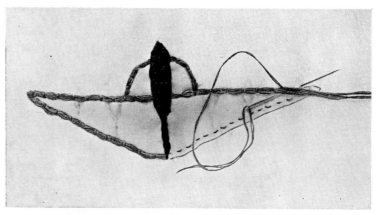

Fig. 15. A simple appliqué for underwear. The edges are held down by couching, which is shown being worked

accumulation of these tiny pieces and is glad to use them up so prettily.

This method is great fun if you like to feel that the whole thing, from beginning to end, is your individual work. Also, you can choose your own colour scheme—an advantage if other furnishings have to be matched.

Some people use two transfers for embroidered appliqué, ironing off one on the background material and cutting up the other so as to stamp its various portions on to different-coloured scraps of material—green for leaves, yellow for flowers and so on. This is a good plan if the design has many small pieces in different colours.

With most large bold designs, however—and appliqué designs *should* be bold—one transfer is enough. Iron this off on the background, then cut up the used transfer and the pieces will serve as paper patterns for cutting the appliqués. When cutting these allow turnings or cut exactly to the stamped lines, according to whether you are using the margin or cut-out methods already described for cretonne appliqué. Generally speaking, unless the

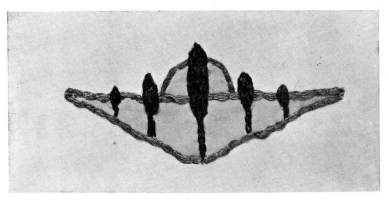

FIG. 16. The completed appliqué seen partly finished in Fig. 15. The trees are embroidered, not applied

various applied portions are quite separate and do not overlap at all, the cut-out method is better here.

Many designs have very thin or tiny portions which are unsuitable for carrying out by applied pieces—stems, for instance, tiny buds or the antennae of butterflies. These are worked in appropriate outline stitches (see Chapter IV) after the appliqués are in place.

In general, work in the same way as for cretonne appliqué. For large applied pieces, which would need very careful tacking, it is often a time-saver to fix them with a dab of paste (the dry kind like "Grip-Fix") in the centre of the appliqué, when much less tacking is needed. Keep the paste clear of the edges, as when it dries it is stiff and hard to sew through.

If two or more applied pieces overlap, remember to place underneath (and consequently to fix and embroider *first*) the part

4—(C.104)

intended to look farthest away in the completed work. This over-lapping most often occurs in picture appliqués containing, say, sky of one colour, a cottage and trees of others and perhaps a fore-ground of a fourth. Here you would start with the sky, add next

the house and trees in the middle distance and over-lap on to these, last of all, the foreground piece.

You will note that in Figs. 15 and 16 the setting sun is overlapped by the horizon and that again by the trees standing near at hand. In this little scene, by the way, the smallest of the trees is too tiny for appliqué (this is only a little dress trimming) and so they are all worked solidly in long-and-short satin-stitch (see page 73).

FIG. 17. This striking sunflower cushion is in blind appliqué; the material, sateen

BLIND APPLIQUÉ

If your tastes run more to plain sewing than to elaborate embroidery, you will like this form of appliqué, introduced to us by em-broideresses of the United States. It is simply appliqués hemmed down, with only certain interior details embroidered, and con-sequently it is very quickly worked. You will find it attractive for large appliqués (like the sunflower cushion design in Fig. 17) which would take a long time to fasten down with an embroidery stitch.

Blind appliqué is also suitable for rather flimsier materials than ordinary appliqué. Sateen was used for the sunflower design and proved most effective with its shiny—but not *too* shiny—

surface. Beautiful bedspreads may be made by blind appliqué. The design may be cut from small-patterned materials as well as from plain ones.

Blind appliqué is extremely simple work. Cut all the appliqué pieces with $\frac{1}{4}$ in. turnings all round. Lay them in position on the stamped background and pin in place, not too near the edge. Then hem each down very neatly with cotton or a single strand of stranded cotton which matches the appliqué (not the background). As you hem, fold in the turnings, using your finger and thumb or poking them under with the needle.

Finally, embroider interior markings, such as the petal veins and centre circles in Fig. 17, in a simple outline stitch.

Where a patterned appliqué is used on a plain ground, it often gives a very handsome result to apply a large design all in one piece, instead of by building up.

INLAY OR DÉCOUPÉ WORK

This French embroidery deserves to be better known, for it is easy, colourful and handsome. It is a kind of reversed appliqué. In appliqué you cut out the parts of a design and apply them to a background. In inlay you cut away the fabric in a pattern or design, to show a different-coloured lining underneath (Fig. 18)— hence its French name, *découpé*, meaning "cut away."

As the material must necessarily be lined, inlay, which looks very like appliqué, as you will see by Fig. 18, is specially suitable for items which need a little weight and thickness, such as runners, chair-backs, lunch mats and table centres. Most appliqué transfers are suitable, particularly those, as in Fig. 18, which have no fine lines to be carried out in stitchery.

Tack the lining and material together all round, with the right side of the lining against the wrong side of the background. The two fabrics should contrast sharply in colour. Beige linen, with a deep red lining, was used for the specimen illustrated, and the embroidery was in red with touches of apple-green (in the French-knot flower centres).

Lining may be throughout or only where the embroidery occurs. The runner in Fig. 18 was embroidered and lined only at each end, the inner edge of the lining being secured to the background with machine hem-stitching to match that round the edges.

Iron off the transfer on to the surface (background) material. With embroidery scissors, carefully poke a hole through a portion of the design through the background only, leaving the lining intact. From this starting point cut away the background along the stamped outlines, so that the lining shows through in the correct shape.

Do not cut away too much at a time, as the cut edges soon fray. First overcast the edges down to the lining, spacing your stitches rather widely, with sewing cotton. Afterwards stitch them down with close buttonholing, covering the overcasting. Both the cotton and embroidery thread used should match the lining.

When cutting out a flower with a centre, like that illustrated, pin down the centre, which is to remain, before cutting the flower petals away. Overcast both flower edges and centre before beginning to embroider, and work the centre, of course, with the buttonhole cord, or purl, to the outside.

A good way to fill such a flower centre is with rings of French knots, growing larger towards the middle, to give a slightly domed effect.

If you prefer geometrical to floral designs, get for your inlay work some glass-towelling (preferably linen) checked with large red or blue squares. Line with the same shade as the squares— casement cloth is a good material for this—then cut away certain squares to form a simple pattern and stitch them down with buttonholing. This is wonderfully effective.

To do a quick job, cut the squares a tiny bit inside their outlines all round, turn in the edges to the checks, and then, as they will not fray, used spaced instead of close buttonholing.

Appliqué and Inlay Stitches

Buttonhole Stitch. The close version, as described below and shown being worked in Fig. 12, is the only embroidery stitch which

FIG. 18. An example of inlay embroidery, with a corner turned
up to show the different coloured lining

finishes edges so firmly that they can be cut away right up to the stitch without fraying. It is sometimes called loop-stitch. Use it for all appliqué and inlay edges in materials which are likely to fray, unless they are held together by being pasted down all over.

Work from left to right. Do not knot the thread, but secure it by making three or four running stitches in the stuff where the buttonholing will cover them. End these on the right side, just where the appliqué edge joins the background. Now from the right side to the wrong, insert your needle through both appliqué and background vertically, the distance away from the edge, inside the appliqué, that the depth of your stitches is to be. Bring it back to the right side just at the appliqué edge. Draw up the thread, being careful to keep it under (behind) the needle.

Insert the needle vertically again just beyond, to make a second stitch parallel with and touching the first, and so continue all along, always holding down the thread under the needle. This gives a solid surface of vertical stitches entirely covering the appliqué edges, with a corded or purled edge lying firmly along the join of the two materials.

Spaced or Open Buttonhole-stitch. Work as above, but leave between the stitches a definite space, usually as wide as the depth of the stitch. As this variation is naturally much quicker to work, but does not stop fraying, use it only when applying non-fraying materials, such as felt or American cloth. Both of these make handsome appliqués, but, of course, neither will wash.

It is also useful in other embroideries for trimming a hem, as in the sachet in Fig. 8. All the buttonhole-stitches in Fig. 19 are variations of spaced buttonholing and are easily copied from the illustration.

Long-and-Short Buttonhole-stitch (Fig. 19, No. III). This simply alternates a long with a short stitch and may be worked either close or spaced. It gives a lighter, less hard effect than close buttonholing, and is pretty in built-up borders (Chapter III) as

well as for appliqué and inlay work. Several variations of it may
be readily followed from Fig. 19.

   Blanket-stitch, though not used for applique or inlay, belongs
to the buttonhole-stitch family and is conveniently given here.

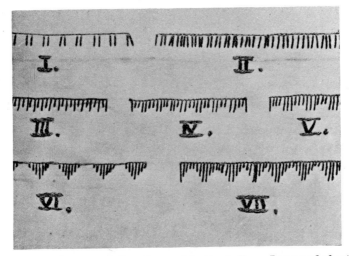

FIG. 19. Seven varieties of spaced buttonholing. Long-and-short
buttonholing is No. III.

It is simply a spaced buttonhole-stitch in which three consecutive
"prongs" are worked into the same hole, the second one straight,
the first and third sloping to meet it. This stitch forms an important part of the wide border in Fig. 3 and also has many pretty
uses as an edging round hems and in building up patterns.

   Couching is not quite such a secure protection against fraying
as buttonhole-stitch, but is much quicker to work and gives a flat
line edge which is very effective on some appliqués (see Fig. 16).
The raw edge should first be secured by overcasting or small
tacking stitches.

   Couching consists of applying a broad, flat thread which covers
well by laying it over the edge and holding it down with tiny

stroke stitches taken across it every $\frac{1}{4}$ in. or $\frac{1}{2}$ in. with a finer thread. Fig. 15 shows six strands of stranded cotton being couched down with two strands. To start, thread the laid (thick) thread into a needle, knot it and bring it through from the wrong side. When couching has been done with a second needle, take the laid thread back to the wrong side and finish it off there.

At corners, simply turn the laid thread till it lies along the new edge. Embroidery wool, used double, with the two thicknesses laid side by side and held down with a shiny thread, is a good couching stitch for cretonne appliqués.

The ships and waves on the cushion in Fig. 10 are couched with chenille, for this stitch is a good, quick one wherever a bold outline is wanted. For rug wool couching, another handsome variation, see Chapter X.

Chapter VI

THE CHARM OF QUILTING

SOME types of embroidery are beautiful, some merely pretty. Others again are striking or delicate or handsome. For quilting I think that there is one adjective and one only—charming. This just describes its lovely play of light and shade and its soft yet definite appearance.

Quilting is one of the simplest of embroideries to work, yet looks expert when done. This is because it is relief work and consequently depends little on colour and even less on stitchery. In fact, it uses only two very simple stitches—back-stitch and running-stitch—and not both of these in any one piece of work!

There are two types of quilting, the English and the Italian.

ENGLISH QUILTING

This, as the names implies, was originally used for the making of quilts. In olden times, when blankets were scarce and expensive and eiderdowns unknown, the poorer housewives would combine economy with warmth by placing several layers of material one over the other and holding them all together with rows or patterns in running-stitch through all the thicknesses. In this way a cosy washable coverlet was made from old or cheap materials, none of which would have been warm enough alone.

In fact, in the days when the Puritans were pioneering in America and able to get new stuffs only once a year, at great cost, from England, quilts always had patchwork top layers pieced together from the tiniest oddments of stuff for which there was no other use.

Usually the two outer layers were of cotton, the middle one being something as warm as possible, yet cheap. In England quilts were filled with sheeps' wool gleaned from the hedges, with warm rags or with thistledown, while in the southern United States fluffy raw cotton from the cotton-fields was used. The patterns used to hold the layers together became more and more beautiful with much practice, and in Wales and the North of England every county had (and even has to this day) its own local designs.

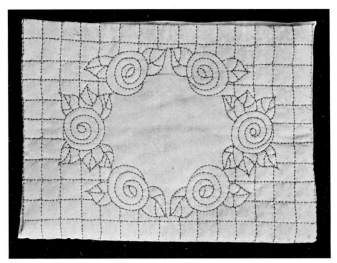

FIG. 20. Nightdress sachet quilted in low relief, with a background of quilted squares

Of recent years, when quilts are no longer essential for warmth, this charming way of quilting has been adapted to modern needs and to smaller items which a home embroideress can quickly finish. It is cosy where warmth is needed, as for tea cosies, hot-water bottle covers, and infants' wadded quilts, and lovely in effect for handbags, cushion covers, nightdress sachets and babies' jackets, bonnets and bibs.

Modern English quilting still consists of three layers, held together by stitchery in a pattern or design. These three layers are—

(1) The visible top (often called the *surface*). For this choose a material both ornamental and soft in texture, such as silk (Fig. 20),

taffeta (Fig. 21), a *soft* cotton (Fig. 22) or linen. Sheeny materials like taffeta give a particularly rich effect.

(2) *The lining* or under layer. This should be of cheap, soft loosely woven cotton, such as cheesecloth or muslin.

(3) The padding, which goes between the other layers and by its thickness produces the characteristic relief effect. Use a layer of cotton-wool for high relief (see the handbag in Fig. 21, with its pronounced light and shade), this layer providing an added amount of warmth. For flatter results, flannel, wincey, domette or any thick, soft, fluffy material is good.

FIG. 21. This taffeta handbag is quilted in back-stitch over a cotton-wool padding

Special quilting transfers are sold, but many intended for other forms of embroidery are just as suitable. The design used may stand alone on a plain background, cover the whole surface, as in Fig. 21, or be backed with a pattern of ruled lines, as in Fig. 20. This last plan enables a small transfer to be used effectively on a large item. If you are adding the lines yourself, remember to rule them out, with faint pencil lines or tailor's chalk, on the design layer before joining it to the other two layers.

Personally, I always transfer the design to, and work from, the top surface—much the most interesting plan, I find. The argument against this is that, if running-stitch is used for quilting, the transfer lines will show between the stitches in the finished work. I find, on the contrary, that the design is only too apt to be rubbed and become almost invisible before working is finished.

However, if you prefer, you can follow what I must admit to be the majority, stamping your design on and working it from the lining side, not the surface.

The chief secret of success in English quilting is good and thorough tacking together of the three layers, so that they cannot possibly shift during the embroidering.

Lay the lining, stamped side outermost, the padding and the surface exactly one over the other in this order and hold with a few pins. Hand-tack all round the edges through the three layers, and then machine-stitch close to the edges, so that the stitches will not show when your work is made up. Then hand-tack across from the middle of each side and end and finally across diagonally from corner to corner. This gives, inside the stitching, eight lines of tacking forming a kind of star. Not much risk of any shifting now!

Old quilting was sometimes chain-stitched, but this is seldom or never seen now. Your choice for the work is between running-stitch and back-stitch (see page 55 and Fig. 27). Work either outwards from the centre or evenly inwards from the corners, *not* from top to bottom or side to side.

As the stitchery is really very unimportant compared with the light and shade effects it produces, it is generally worked in a fine thread or sewing silk which exactly matches the surface, as in Fig. 21. But if you prefer, especially when you are using only a thin padding, you can embroider in a darker tone (Fig. 20), in black (Fig. 22) or each part of the design in a different appropriate colour.

Stab your stitches back and forth, as, if you try to run two or three at once, with so much thickness you are likely not to catch the under layer securely.

When all quilting is finished, remove the tackings and press *very lightly* on the wrong side with the work laid on a thick ironing blanket. As some quilting will not even stand this amount of pressing, which is not enough to take out heavy creases, any folds or crumples in the surface should always be ironed out *before* it is tacked to the remaining layers.

Pattern Quilting

I give this name to a variation of English quilting which I evolved some years ago. Work it in all ways as previously described, but, instead of using a transfer, employ the surface of a material already patterned or printed with a design and quilt the outlines of this or round it.

FIG. 22. Pattern quilting in black and green running-stitch on a soft cotton

Fig. 22 shows one corner of a cotton handkerchief, which was printed with a black and green floral design and quilted in running-stitch in the same shades. Afterwards it was made up, with a second handkerchief as a backing, into a handkerchief sachet.

When the surface has widely spaced sprays or motifs too small for quilting, each can be effectively enclosed in a circle or a diamond and these connected up to form a simple geometrical pattern.

This form of quilting has the advantage of contrasting colourings and it gives different designs from those obtainable in transfers.

Italian or Corded Quilting

No pretence to warmth is made by this delightful type of quilting. It is purely ornamental. Instead of having the whole of the work in relief, the outlines of the design only are raised or corded. It gives a rich yet delicate effect for adorning many household articles and is also sometimes in fashion in the dress world, for handbags and the hems of evening gowns or dressing gowns.

Italian quilting, by the way, washes quite well.

FIG. 23. Organdie cushion cover in Italian quilting, padded with
8-ply wool

Buy a special Italian quilting transfer with double outlines or make a simple one of your own with various-sized circles and straight lines, of the kind shown on the artificial silk pram cover in Fig. 25.

No interlining is needed. Use the same materials, except linen, as for English quilting; organdie, voile and crêpe de Chine are also excellent as surface fabrics. Tack the top and lining together as described for the English type.

Work the whole design through both layers in self-coloured running-stitch. Turn the work to the wrong side, and then with your fine-pointed embroidery scissors poke a hole, *through the lining only*, into one of the channels formed by the double lines of stitchery. With a bodkin thread four thicknesses of embroidery wool right through the channel, so that the design outline is softly padded and raised.

If you come to the end of your wool, or reach a turn where the

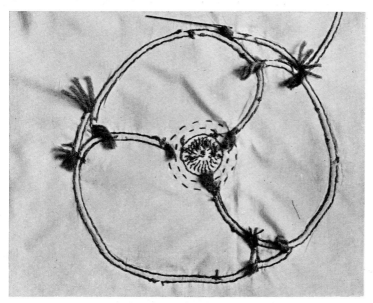

FIG. 24. Italian quilting (wrong side) showing wool being run through the double outlines

bodkin cannot pass, bring the wool out through another hole made in the same way (as in the upper part of Fig. 24), and start afresh through the same hole with a new length. Thread the entire design in this way, and the lining side will give the effect seen in Fig. 24, while the surface has the whole design delicately raised and emphasized, as in Figs. 23 and 25.

The latter shows the usual one-tone effect. To the cushion cover in Fig. 23 gay colour is also added, by using as a surface a pale-tinted organdie and doing the threading with a much more vivid shade so that it shows, a little subdued, through the transparent material.

Details, such as the eyes and markings of the fishes, are worked in outline stitches.

If you have in the house left-overs of either thin rug wool or eight-ply wool, you can pad with a single thickness of either of

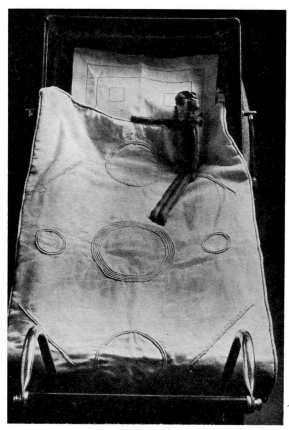

FIG. 25. This Italian quilted pram cover has a simple design
made with plates and a ruler

these instead of using embroidery wool. Remember, though, that the double outlines of transfers are not usually wide enough for the eight-ply wool, so the transfer should be stamped on the lining and one row of stitchery worked outside the marked line to increase the size of the channels. This was done for the fish outlines in Fig. 23.

If the wrong side of the quilting will show, as for the pram cover in Fig. 25 or the flap of a night-dress sachet, line this neatly with thin silk to hide the holes and ends of wool.

There is another very neat way of quilting and padding so that there are no holes or ends to conceal and the wrong side is as tidy as the right side. This, though, can only be used when the design is one made up of enclosed spaces of various shapes, like the circles (Fig. 25) and fishes (Fig. 23).

To work this way, tack together the two layers of material only in the very centre, pinning them instead at the corners. Stitch all round the *inside* outline of each space. Remove the pins and lay the padding wool between the two layers, as close up to the stitching as possible. Fold back the surface, tack it securely to the lining and work the second line of quilting to hold the wool in place.

SHADOW QUILTING

This is very modern embroidery, with no history behind it, so that you will like it if you enjoy being right up to date! It combines boldness with delicacy in a very charming way.

The idea, as clearly seen in Fig. 26, is first to work solid, vividly coloured embroidery on one material, and then to veil it with a pale, transparent second fabric. This is quilted down to the embroidery by the embroidered outlines being sewn round, through both materials, with back-stitch. The photograph shows, to the left, the original solid embroidery; on the right is the softer finished effect when this has cherry-coloured organdie quilted over its outlines.

This specimen was embroidered on a soft linen, and, as you will see, the effect is good. For more blurred results, the under material is usually of the fluffy type used for interlining in English quilting —say, wincey or delaine. As these fabrics are warm and washable, shadow quilting makes one of the prettiest of embroideries for babies' little jackets and bonnets. It is also delicately beautiful

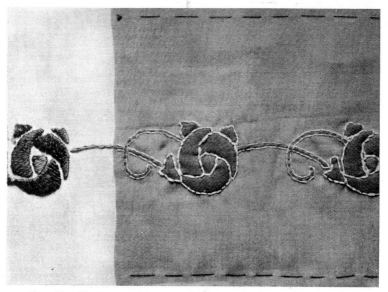

FIG. 26. Shadow quilting: *Left*, the embroidered under layer; *Right*, organdie laid over and back-stitched down

for dressing jackets, cot and pram covers, sachets and evening handbags.

The embroidery on the under material must be worked solidly in satin-stitch (page 73) or Roumanian-stitch (page 97). Use very bright, strong colours, as these will be much subdued by the veiling material, which may be organdie or, for very luxurious use when washing will not be required, georgette or ninon.

Exquisite colour effects are possible by varying and mingling the tones of the under material, the embroidery, the veiling fabric and the quilting thread in various ways. These may match, tone or contrast in a hundred fascinating variations. Make your own experiments with scraps of stuff and you will be delighted with the lovely results obtainable.

When quilting stems or fine parts of the work use a thinner

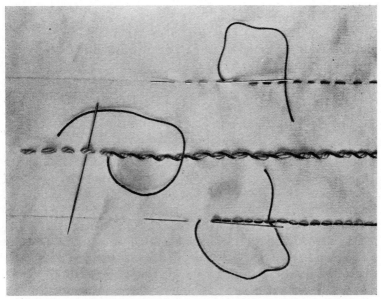

FIG. 27. Quilting stitches: *Top*, running-stitch; *Middle*, overcast running-stitching; *Bottom*, back-stitch

thread than for the larger portions. In Fig. 26 the roses were quilted with white *Coton à broder*, the slender stems with only a single strand of white stranded cotton.

QUILTING STITCHES

Only two are ever used in modern quilting—running-stitch and back-stitch.

Running-stitch (Fig. 27, top), is the plain sewing stitch of that name. Work from right to left. Bring the needle through from the wrong side and pick up a horizontal stitch to the left—say

$\frac{1}{8}$ in. long. Re-insert the needle $\frac{1}{8}$ in. farther along to take up another $\frac{1}{8}$-in. long stitch and so continue, so that stitches of equal length lie alternately on each side of the stuff. In plain sewing and outline embroideries several stitches are taken on the needle at once, as shown, but for most quilting one stitch only can be taken at a time, the needle being stabbed back and forth.

Back-stitch (Fig. 27, bottom) is also a plain sewing stitch. Begin by making a running-stitch backwards. But when putting the needle through to the wrong side, after making the first stitch, carry it under not only the stitch made but a space equal in length to that stitch, as in the photograph. Bring it up, fill up the space by taking a backward stitch, and so continue, always coming up a stitch's length to the left of the stitch and then filling the space with a backward stitch.

Back-stitch naturally quilts more slowly than running stitch, but it is preferred sometimes in English and Italian quilting for its heavier effect, especially when the outline contrasts in colour with the surface. Use it always in shadow quilting. Here I find it looks best if worked, not as given above, but as two rows of running-stitch, the second filling in the spaces left by the first.

Overcast Running-stitch (Fig. 27, middle) is not a quilting stitch, but is conveniently described here with running-stitch, of which it is a variation. Work a line of running-stitch in one colour, then whip over each stitch, always from above downwards, with a second shade. The needle when whipping goes behind the running-stitch but not through the fabric. This is a good stitch where a noticeable outline is wanted or as a simple border trimming for children's clothes.

Wave-stitch is another fancy running-stitch useful for borders and simple trimmings. Work as for the overcast running-stitch, but take the second thread alternately into the running-stitches from above and below, so that a curved outline, rather like waves or scallops, is formed. Waves in a design are often worked this way, the whipping stitches being left rather loose to give a pronounced curve. It is also pretty to hold down tucks decoratively.

Chapter VII

DARNED EMBROIDERIES

THE previous chapter ended with running-stitch and one or
two of its variations—appropriately enough, for now we come
to embroideries which are carried out in darning-stitch, and, as, of
course, you know, darning is only a running-stitch dressed up a
little and arranged in tidy rows!

You would hardly think that such a very simple, almost
uninteresting, stitch would lend itself to the very pretty decora-
tions it actually does. Here are some of the most useful and
effective. All are quick and easy to work and have the advantage
of washing well.

Darning on Huckaback

Huckaback has a natural texture which simply cries out for
decoration in darning. It has a clear weave which is easily followed
and threads at regular intervals that lie on the surface and are
readily picked up by a darning stitch.

So if you have fresh, firm towels to embroider, here is your
chance! They will have just the right amount of adornment and
colour if you provide the important end of each with a strip pattern
darned by eye into the surface threads.

You will find it easy and thrilling to invent your own patterns,
either drawing them roughly first on squared paper or making
them up as you go along. Start by copying the simple two-colour
zigzag border in Fig. 28, and by the time that is finished you will
be bursting with ideas of your own!

Darn with a fairly thick (or a thin doubled) thread, almost
entirely on the surface, so that practically the whole of the pattern
is on the right side. This effect is easily gained by letting the
thread lie and keeping it in place merely by picking up the fine
surface threads of the huckaback.

The pattern is a simple one. Starting 1 in. from a side edge of the towel, darn three parallel zigzag rows across, one below the other, following the surface threads up and down in connecting V's in, say, deep blue. Then darn three more rows in light blue,

FIG. 28. Two-tone zig-zag border decoratively darned on a huckaback towel

exactly similar to the first except that they go up where the dark ones go down and *vice versa*. This gives diamond spaces between the two colours; fill each of these with a pale darned diamond, with a dot (French knot) at its centre.

Complete the border with three more rows of dark blue, and dark blue diamonds to fill the spaces between them and the light blues.

The basket weave pattern in Fig. 34 is also suitable for huckaback.

You need not confine yourself to geometrical patterns, for

quaint little house and tree designs look very well. They are quite easy to darn in by eye, as they are nearly all straight lines. If you prefer, draw first on squared paper a little house of the kind children draw; then copy this on the huckaback in appropriate colours—red walls, blue roof, green trees and so on. The result is especially quaint for nursery use.

The beautiful modern huckabacks in pastel colours are worth using, not only for towels, but for chair-backs, bedside table mats and duchesse sets. To finish the edges of these in keeping with their darned designs, fringe them out up to a line of machine stitching one inch away from each edge or fold the hems and darn these instead of hemming them.

DARNED SWAB CUSHIONS

Would you believe that an ordinary sixpenny swab from Woolworth's, darned in bright colours in the simplest of running-stitches, could make such an effective cushion cover as that shown in Fig. 29? Yes, it is not only possible, but very easy and cheap to fashion.

Choose the kind of square swab which has a loose but regular weave, of thick cotton one way, held together by finer threads in the reverse direction. Darn a triangle in each corner and a diamond in the centre, in bright blue and bright red or any other two vivid colours which show up brilliantly against the drab of the swab.

The simple darning-stitch used is chain darning, described on page 65.

Make up the cushion with another swab, darned to match in another design but the same stitch, or left quite plain, as a backing. You will find it particularly suitable for garden or nursery use.

DARNING ON NET

The large square mesh of curtain net may be darned in wools or thick cotton threads to give decoration and colour along the hems of short glass curtains (Fig. 30) or on runners or transparent net bed-spreads. The most suitable designs are geometrical borders of much the same kind as those used for huckaback darning; count them out on the squares as you work.

Whatever wool or thread is used, it must be thick enough, when worked either single or double, to fill the mesh completely.

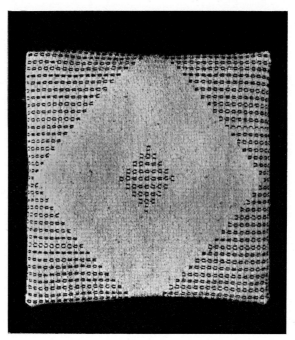

Fig. 29. Cushion cover made from a swab adorned with chain darning

For some large meshes the very thick, soft eight-ply wool is excellent; for more ordinary sizes, embroidery wool used double or the thicker cotton threads are suitable. Silk is too soft to fill well.

Choose bold, simple designs for curtain net and work them in few but vivid colours. A border at the bottom of a curtain or the end of a runner will always be well placed. Do not make a hem,

but turn up singly double the hem width. Leave the bottom part
as it is to give the hem effect, and then begin the border, darning
its first few rows through both the article itself and the top part
of the turn, so that the turn is held firmly in place. Or turn up

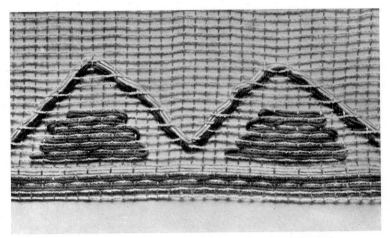

Fig. 30. Part of a net curtain border, darned in thick cotton,
used double

more narrowly and start the darning one mesh from the edge as
in Fig. 30.

Never begin with a knot. A much neater plan is to darn in the
new thread among the last few squares of the old, where it will be
lost to sight.

For finer articles, such as wedding or confirmation veils, net
hems on underwear or modesty vests, dress net may be darned
with a suitable number of strands of stranded cotton. This is
usually kept to an all-white or a one-colour effect and can be very
dainty and lacy. The fine mesh is trying to count, but transfers
may be obtained for this kind of darning. A transfer will not iron
off on net; tack it behind the net so that it will show through
the mesh. Embroider through both net and paper and afterwards
gently tear the paper away.

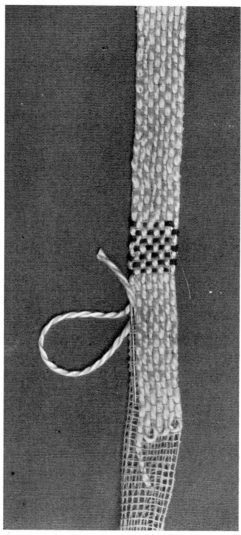

FIG. 31. Underwear shoulder strap may
be darned solidly on doubled net

If you have plenty of patience, you can even darn net completely over the whole surface with wool to form a warm yet strong hand-made fabric for fashioning into little house-coats, capes or cushion covers. Fig. 31, which shows a darned net shoulder strap, illustrates the idea on a small scale.

To give the strap strength, the net is cut more than twice the width needed and folded to give a double thickness $\frac{1}{2}$ in. to $\frac{3}{4}$ in. wide. Darn through all thicknesses straight up and down, as when darning a stocking, using a thick, soft embroidery cotton such as Anchor Flox, as wool is not suited to the constant washing needed for underwear.

The band of coloured cross-darning is purely for ornament and may be placed at regular intervals along the strap or merely in front a little above the top of the "undie." Such straps are quickly made, wear well and do not easily slip. Hat-bands may be darned (in wool) in the same way.

When a whole garment is being made, cut it out first in the net, with turnings; it will cut most easily if it is first tacked to tissue paper and the two are cut together. Join the main seams, and then darn all over, up and down one way only or in some simple all-over pattern. Suitable patterns can often be adapted from cross-stitch or tapestry, by the way (see Chapter XIII). Darn sleeves before making them up and setting them in. Afterwards line the garment with thin silk to neaten the wrong side.

FIG. 32. A flower may be outlined and lightly filled in with darning-stitch

DARNING—MISCELLANEOUS USES

Darning is a quick and pretty aid to the home embroideress in all sorts of minor ways. In fact, as you will see, it is most decidedly a stitch to cultivate.

For borders, built up from simple stitches as explained in Chapter III, it is very useful indeed. Note its effectiveness as an edging to the wool-on-linen panel in Fig. 5, for instance, while as a quickly worked, coloured hem it gives an attractive appearance to the mat in Fig. 9. If you want a border or band trimming entirely in darning, a pretty two-colour one is shown in Fig. 34 and described fully on page 66. This is called the basket-stitch, from its likeness to the weave of a basket.

For outlining, darning-stitch gives quick results. I possess a tea-table set which is mostly worked in this stitch—very strikingly.

The blue linen appliqué baskets which hold the little tea napkins have their edges turned in singly and then are run or darned into place—a much more rapid method than buttonhole-stitching. The flower outlines (one is shown in Fig. 32) are worked with two

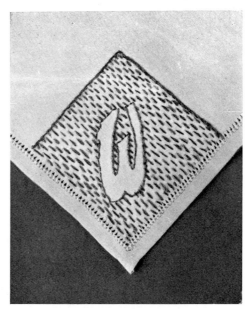

FIG. 33. One-way darning in close rows
forms a good background

lines of darning. The first, in orange, leaves spaces which are filled by the second line in yellow. This second line, however, is run just inside the first, so that the two rows of stitches, instead of forming together one smooth line of back-stitch, give a broken and rather more noticeable edge.

As a light filling, spaced rows of darning (Fig. 32) are quickly worked and pretty. They give more "body" than simple out-lines, but take much less time and thread than satin-stitch. Keep the darning running all one way across a flower, not straight across or down each petal, as the latter gives a fidgety result.

As a background, darning has the same advantages as for a filling—a definite look without solidity. Fig. 33 shows this use of

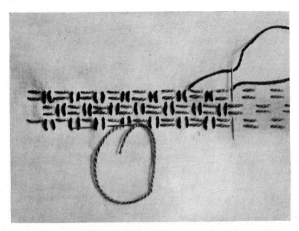

Fig. 34. Basket-stitch darning in two colours

it to throw up an initial simply outlined in back-stitching. Note that the stitches run with the weave of the material, not at right-angles to the letter, which is on the diagonal.

Darning Stitches

The ordinary darning-stitch, as I have said, is merely running-stitch (page 55) taken in rows. These may run with the stitches exactly parallel in each row (Fig. 34), alternating (Figs. 29 and 33), or crossing at right-angles (the coloured part in Fig. 31).

Here are some pretty variations of the stitch.

Chain Darning (used for the cushion cover in Fig. 29). This stitch consists of three rows of darning worked quite close together. Work one row in one colour, and then a second row, its stitches alternating with the first, in a second colour. For the third row repeat the stitches as in the first row, again using the first colour.

In the cushion cover illustrated the first and third rows in each chain are in scarlet, the second row in royal blue.

Basket-stitch (Fig. 34) is a pattern built up entirely in darning-stitch. Run rows of horizontal stitches first in pairs, making the stitches the same size as the spaces between them. With a second colour work a pair of *upright* darning-stitches in every space between the horizontal ones. The border can be any width wanted, from two horizontal pairs of rows wide upwards.

Link Darning, rather like an elongated version of chain darning, finishes the hem of the table-cloth in Fig. 61, page 105. Begin as for basket weave, with two parallel rows of darning, and the stitches matched, and rather longer than the spaces. Then fill each space with a cross-stitch (page 139).

Chapter VIII
BRODERIE ANGLAISE (EYELET WORK)

DO you want a beautiful open-work embroidery which will outlast the fabric on which it is worked, wash everlastingly and always look fresh and good? Then you cannot do better than work a piece of *broderie anglaise*, or eyelet work, to give it its English name.

As this embroidery, owing to the wearing and washing qualities just mentioned, was chiefly used for things perpetually being laundered, such as household linen and underwear, it used to be all-white work. Consequently, when the modern craze for colour came in, *broderie anglaise* was rather pushed on one side and forgotten.

But now it is very decidedly "in" again. For one thing it has been charmingly adapted to colour, as you see by Figs. 36 and 37. For another, even if it remains all snowy, we have found that a white note is a very pleasant contrast to so many rainbow tints.

For household linen often in the wash-tub there is no embroidery to equal it, and it is always in vogue to embellish such things as sheets, pillow-slips, tray and table-cloths, lunch sets or doyleys. When cotton and linen underwear was in fashion *broderie anglaise* was much used for this, but it needs a fairly thick, firm fabric and does not take so kindly to modern diaphanous silks.

As its English name, eyelet work, suggests, its characteristic feature is its numerous pierced holes known as eyelets. These are most often round, but sometimes oval or leaf-shaped. A round eyelet makes a realistic little berry, and so most *broderie anglaise* designs are of the berry and narrow leaf type, as you will see by the illustrations in this chapter.

In Madeira or stiletto embroidery, worked by peasant women in the island of Madeira, the entire design is carried out in eyelets pierced with a stiletto or cut. This is not often done by English embroideresses, who prefer *broderie anglaise* proper, which varies the eyelets with satin-stitched portions; and I think that they are right in doing so. For while the eyelets look lovely against a dark polished background, such as a dining table, their darkness is also

FIG. 35. Linen mat in simple eyelet work, with scalloped edge

most effectively thrown up by the solid whiteness of the satin-stitched parts. This contrast is well shown in Fig. 35.

In addition to satin-stitch, outline, cord and punch stitches are sometimes used. For instance, the stems are outline-stitched in Fig. 37.

You will notice that the mat in Fig. 35 and the tray-cloth in Fig. 38 have their edges worked in scalloping, a very favourite and appropriate finish for eyelet work (see Chapter IX). If you want an edge that takes less time, hem-stitched hems always look well. A particularly pretty and easy hem-stitch (described in Chapter XII under "Drawn-Thread Work") is used for the breakfast set in Figs. 36 and 37.

As *broderie anglaise* is rather slow work until you get used to it, I should advise you to make your first attempt on something quite small—a little mat, a crisp white collar for a dark dress or an initial on a piece of house linen (see Chapter XI for initials).

FIG. 36. Green linen breakfast set, embroidered with white eyelets and yellow satin-stitch

The materials which best take *broderie anglaise* are substantial, closely woven ones such as linen, sheeting, Tarantulle, madapolam and piqué—this last for dress items. Use a firm, non-shiny embroidery cotton.

When you want to work in colours, you will find that a white or pale design embroidered on a clear colour is more effective than a white background with coloured embroidery. Take the breakfast set in Fig. 36. This is of blue-green linen, with white eyelet berries and the few star-like satin-stitched flowers worked in pale yellow.

Solid-looking dots are a feature of *broderie anglaise*. Carry them out in satin-stitch, which may also be used for leaves. Stems cannot be eyeletted, so work them in outline or cord stitch.

When doing all-white *broderie anglaise*, you may find that your eyes tire from the lack of contrast. If so, take a tip from Madeira

Fɪɢ. 37. Detail of the breakfast set in Fig. 36. Notice the novel hem-stitched edge

women, and dip your working thread in a little blue so that it shows up clearly against the white background. This is much more restful to the eyes, and the blue shade gives place to all-white as soon as the work is laundered.

Eyeletting is apt to mean a much-pricked finger. You can avoid this, and at the same time soothe the eyes, if you wrap a strip of green American cloth round the left forefinger, so that it comes under the eyelet being made.

Take pains with your work. As very few stitches are used, much depends on having a good design and working it with care.

Eyelets are made with the simplest stitches, but a certain amount of practice is needed to get them well rounded and so firm that they will wash well. Practise this on oddments of stuff—*not* on a regular piece of embroidery.

FIG. 38. A tray-cloth combining *broderie anglaise* and cut-work, and a cosy in felt appliqué, beautify this tea-table

BRODERIE ANGLAISE STITCHES

Eyelets are, of course, the most important. The majority of these are round—in fact, many pieces of work contain no others. They are also the easiest shape to make, so get your hand in with these first of all.

Round Eyelets (Fig. 39, *A*) are indicated on the transfer by small circles. Outline each circle with running-stitch to give a slight firmness and roundness to the edge. With your embroidery stiletto, pierce the hole inside the running-stitches, as shown, but do not cut away any of the raw edges inside the hole. Whip closely and tightly over and over the run edge all round the hole. Whipping, by the way, is simply a close, tight overcasting, as you see by Fig. 39, *A*. Pull each stitch firmly to give a clear-cut round hole and, as you whip, catch in the raw edges made by the piercing.

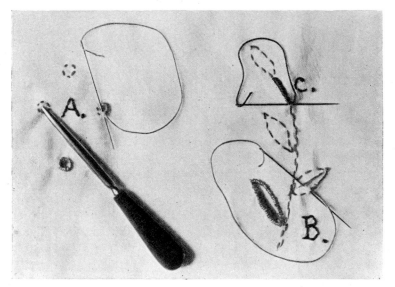

FIG. 39. *Broderie anglaise.* Stages of making: *A*, round eyelets, and *B*, oval eyelets; *C*, cord-stitch

Oval or Leaf-shaped Eyelets (Fig. 39, *B*) should first be outlined with running-stitch as described for the round shape above. Then cut with your fine embroidery scissors from one end of the oval to the other, down its centre. Whip tightly all round, whipping in all raw edges (again, do not cut these away) as you go.

Satin-stitch (Fig. 40) comes after eyelets in importance for *broderie anglaise,* but it is also so greatly used for many other types of embroidery that in the illustration I have shown one of its general uses, in colour, instead of as a definite eyelet-work stitch, when it will usually be in white.

Satin-stitch is very simple and is best described by saying that it is a series of stroke-stitches (see page 26) lying smoothly side by side and touching, so that they cover the whole surface of the part of the design being embroidered. They are worked across the

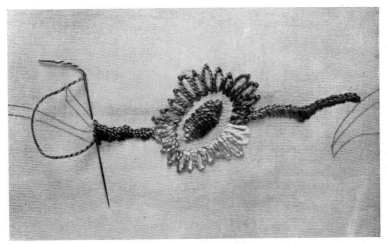

FIG. 40. How satin-stitch is worked

outlines the *short* way (Fig. 40) because long satin-stitches, like stroke-stitches, would be apt to catch in things in wear. They may be *slanted* across, however, if this gives a better effect and does not make the stitches too long. They are often worked thus for narrow leaves.

Examples of this stitch used in various types of embroidery are shown in Figs. 9 (the bow of ribbon), 26 (the roses on the under layer of linen), 37 (the daisy-like flower), 51 (flowers and leaves), 59 (monogram) and 87 (block markings on the bowl).

Padded Satin-stitch, seen being worked in Fig. 81, is mostly used for *broderie anglaise*, rather than the simple variety given above, as the padding produces a very hard-wearing, well-raised effect, which contrasts delightfully with the sunken look of the eyelets. Work this just as for satin-stitch, but first pad the parts to be covered with chain-stitch (page 107), working this in rows or coils one inside the other to fill the space, if the latter is too wide to be padded with a single line. For narrow outlines or when a rather flatter effect is wanted, padding may be done with running-stitch instead.

Cord-stitch (Fig. 39, *C*), a variation of padded satin-stitch, is often used in *broderie anglaise* for working fine stems, tendrils, etc. It gives a very slender but well raised and noticeable outline. The fine stems in Fig. 96 are worked in this stitch, by which you will see that its use is not confined to eyelet work. In fact, it is a favourite stitch for joining net hems or lace to underwear, and you will also be glad of it sometimes in various coloured embroideries.

Other names for this stitch are roll or fine satin-stitch.

Pad the line to be worked with one, two or three rows of fine running-stitches, according to its width. Then satin-stitch closely over them, at right-angles to the running-stitches, making the satin-stitches only just long enough to cover the padding and pulling them rather tight. Or the satin-stitch may be worked over a laid thread.

Punch, Lace, Pin or Turkey-stitch (it has all these names) is an open-work stitch which is sometimes used in rather elaborate *broderie anglaise*, or in cut-work (see next chapter) as an open-work filling for a flower or motif. The chances are that you will not do any embroidery of these two kinds which is complicated enough to need this stitch, but I am including it because it is also such a charming one for joining lace to underwear or evening handker-chiefs in an open-work stitch. It is rather slow to do, but, unlike hem-stitching, does not depend on the drawing of threads. You can therefore use it round curves and for all sorts of fancy shapes.

Try it also for working initials (Chapter XI) or butterfly or bow-of-ribbon motifs on lingerie. These look fairy-like when out-lined in a series of fine holes by means of punch-stitch.

In order to pierce the holes, the very large needle known as a punch needle (page 41) must be used. Tie into this a fine thread, such as ordinary sewing silk or a single strand of stranded cotton.

This is a double back-stitch piercing the material with a double line of holes in one operation. Lightly mark in pencil (or merely

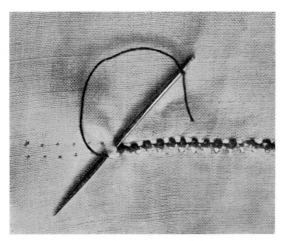

FIG. 41. Punch or lace-stitch is worked with a huge
punch needle

imagine, if you are a practised worker) a double line of dots, as to the left in Fig. 41. They should be a trifle under $\frac{1}{8}$ in. apart, both from each other and between the two rows.

Now mentally number the first four (two in each row) round in a square in a counter-clockwise direction, thus—

3 2

4 1

Work from right to left. Bring the needle out from the wrong side (after securing the fine thread so that it cannot work through the large hole made by the needle), and back-stitch straight upwards to Hole 2, twice. The second time take the needle diagonally downwards to Hole 4 (Fig. 41 shows it in this position), and back-stitch twice from there diagonally upwards back to

Hole 2. The second time take the needle horizontally forward to Hole 3 and back-stitch twice from there into Hole 2. The second time bring the needle out in Hole 4.

This completes a unit of stitches. Now remember Hole 4, in which the needle is, and call it Hole 1. This gives you a fresh group of four holes, two old and two new, to work in the same way. Continue so all along.

Pull every stitch tightly in order to make a clear hole. If you are punch-stitching lace to material, first tack the lace to the fabric so that its straight edge runs along just between the two lines of dots. In this way every stitch into the upper line will secure lace and material together.

When using punch-stitch as a filling, work it in continuous rows covering the whole space.

CHAPTER IX

CUT-WORK AND BUTTONHOLED EMBROIDERY

CUT-WORK may be described as embroidery's nearest approach to lace-making. You have only to look at the beautiful cloth in Fig. 42 to see the likeness to lace, though, of course, in a comparatively bold and heavy form. In spite of the resemblance, actually the methods of work in the two forms are directly opposite ones. Lace patterns are built up thread by thread out of thin air, so to speak; whereas in cut-work we take a solid piece of material and from it remove enough pieces, by cutting, to throw up the embroidered pattern against a background of spaces—or openwork. These background spaces are then given strength and held together, in many cases, by fine buttonholed threads—called bars —being thrown across them.

This exquisite embroidery is a kind of cousin of *broderie anglaise*. Both are worked very largely in all-white, and cut-work is as perfect as eyelet work for household linens, since it wears and washes almost equally well. The same fabrics and threads also suit them both.

In fact, they have so many similarities that there is a modern fashion for combining them in one item. The tray-cloth in Fig. 38 is an example of this wedding of the two, for the design shows the typical berry sprays and satin-stitched dots of *broderie anglaise*, and also the equally typical cut-work bars. But actually, though I show you this blend as a matter of interest, I should strongly advise you to work either eyelets or cut-work on a given item, but not *both*. Each type of embroidery has its own strongly marked characteristics and each is well able to stand alone. In my opinion nothing is gained by combining the two types and a good deal of their individuality is lost. Also, it is difficult to find a transfer equally suitable for both.

Cut-work is an exquisite decoration for household linens such as table and tray-cloths, sheet shams and pillow-slips, lunch mats, handkerchief sachets and linen guest towels. It also makes a fairy-like trimming for silken underwear.

It is not necessary, of course, to do the immense amount of work involved in such an item as the cloth in Fig. 42. If you have time and patience to undertake anything so exquisite, no doubt it will be handed down in your family as a treasured heirloom! But it is far more likely that you will only want to work a small spray

FIG. 42. A very beautiful table-cloth in Richelieu cut-work

or motif of the type shown in Fig. 43, and this illustration shows
how wonderfully effective such a spray can be.

Despite its lacy look, there is a sort of vigorous independence
about cut-work which is well shown when a little of the embroidery

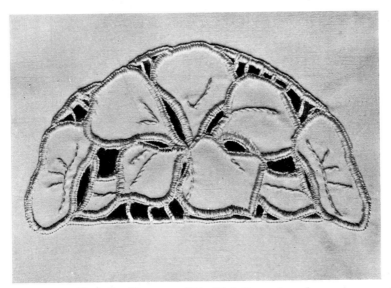

FIG. 43. Flower motif in Richelieu cut-work

has plenty of plain material round it as a background. Such
detached motifs have the advantage that they are quite quickly
worked.

As cut-work is carried out almost entirely in buttonhole-stitch,
a scalloped edge, as on the cloth in Fig. 42, is the most appropriate
hem finish. Scalloping, of course, is merely close buttonhole-
stitch worked round a series of curves or scallops, with the material
outside it cut away (Fig. 44). Sometimes—with many lunch mat
designs, for instance—a portion of the design itself forms a more
or less scalloped edge. (See Fig. 45.)

Hem-stitching is quicker, but not nearly so effective a hem

finish for this embroidery. If you *do* use hem-stitching, the Italian form (page 114) is the most suitable.

Cut-work may be made with bars, when it is often called Richelieu work; or without them—Roman cut-work. The first way gives the delicate, lace-like look, as in Figs. 42 and 43.

In Roman cut-work narrow parts of the design, such as stems, act as bars or else the spaces are small enough to need none. As the bars are the most difficult part of cut-work, the Roman kind is easier for a first attempt and gives bolder results. (Fig. 45.)

For either type, use a proper cut-work transfer. If it has bars, these will be shown on it as single lines crossing the spaces.

When choosing your embroidery thread, remember that this work is far prettier if done all in one colour, especially in white, or with the thread only a trifle darker or lighter than the stuff. The reason is simple. Cut-work owes its charm to the contrast between the pale material and stitchery and the dark cut-away spaces. The introduction of a second colour spoils this contrast and muddles the shapes of the cut-away parts.

Iron the transfer on to the material. Then, to avoid any cutting mistakes later, before you start embroidering look carefully over the design, and mark with a pencil cross each space which is to be cut away.

Richelieu Cut-work

To give a bold, firm edge to the outlines, first pad just inside them with running-stitches (Fig. 46, *A*). Run one way and then return, alternating the stitches, so that you have a double line of padding. While putting in the running-stitch, as you come to each mark for a bar, make a back-stitch just inside the outline, and then lay a long stitch across the bar mark and into the edge opposite. Pull quite taut and secure with another tiny back-stitch; then return with a second stitch across and lying close alongside the first. Back-stitch again, and then continue with the running-stitch.

This is my own working plan. Some people, however, prefer to

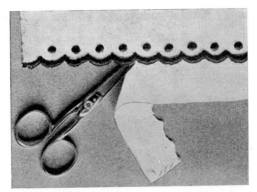

FIG. 44. Scalloping worked in close buttonhole-stitch, with surplus material being cut away

FIG. 45. This linen vase mat is in Roman cut-work, which has no bars

put in the whole of the bars after the rest of the design is finished. So you should try both methods and decide which one *you* prefer.

When the padding and bar lines are completed, work all the outlines, over the running-stitches, in close, firm buttonhole-

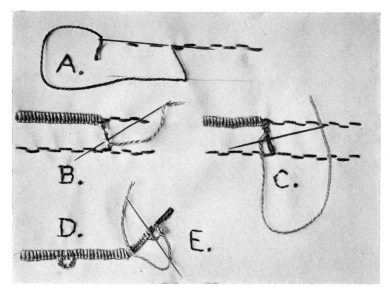

Fig. 46. Cut-work details: *A*, padding outlines with running-stitch; *B*, working overcast bar; *C*, working buttonholed bar; *D*, completed picot; *E*, making it

stitch, as in Fig. 43. Remember that round the spaces the corded edge (called the purl) of the buttonholing must always come *against* the space, not away from it; otherwise it will not hold when cutting away is done.

As with the padding, when you reach each laid bar, work it, or leave all bars to the end if you prefer it. To work a bar, buttonhole closely all along, over both the laid threads together, but not into the stuff, which later is to be cut away (Fig. 46, *C*).

Though buttonholed bars are the most usual, they may be made, if preferred, by either overcasting or needle-weaving.

Overcast or Twisted Bars. Lay one thread only as already described. Return by overcasting closely over this thread all along (Fig. 46, *B*). This makes a fine bar without very much strength.

Woven Bars. Lay either two or four threads side by side and weave these as explained on page 122 for needle-weaving, though needle-weaving, of course, is done into the threads of the material instead of on added ones. The bar thus made is strong and rather thick.

Work small interior markings, such as stamens or veins on leaves, in simple outline stitches. In large designs veins are effective in triangular feather-stitch, and petals and flower centres may be filled with a powdering of seed-stitch. Bars may have picots added. For these stitches see page 86.

Just a hint! Be careful, when moving from one part of a cut-work design to another, not to take the thread across any future open space, or it will show when you cut away. Instead, carry it along on the wrong side through a buttonholed edge, or finish off and start again.

When all embroidery is done—not before, please!—use your sharp embroidery scissors (as shown in Fig. 44 for scalloping) to cut away the material in the marked spaces. Cut carefully, close up to the buttonhole purl, especially in corners, but not cutting anywhere through it or the bars.

It is a good plan to launder the work, or at any rate to damp and press it, *before* doing any cutting away, as then it is much less inclined to develop "whiskers" after the first washing. However, this certainly does destroy the freshness of the work a little, so that you may prefer merely to press it before cutting.

Roman Cut-work

Everything already said about Richelieu work applies equally to this, except that there are, of course, no bars to add (see Fig. 45).

There is one additional point not met with in Richelieu work. If part of the design forming a bar is too narrow to have button-holing worked along each edge. as occasionally happens, and yet each edge comes next to a space, you may think that you are in Queer Street! Not at all. First buttonhole with the purl along one edge, spacing your stitches a little. Then repeat with the purl along the second edge, this time working into the spaces between the first row of stitches.

FIG. 47. This serviette ring is worked almost entirely in spaced buttonhole-stitch

It may happen sometimes that you want to do bar cut-work but have only a Roman cut-work transfer. Iron this off in the interior of the stuff (not up to an edge). Then confine it rather closely in an oval, circle or diamond or other appropriate shape which touches the design in places and in others can be connected to it by bars, and work as for Richelieu cutwork. This method was used in the motif in Fig. 43, which began life minus its bars and semi-circular outline.

BUTTONHOLED EMBROIDERIES

Buttonholing is such a useful and decorative stitch that it plays the leading part in various embroideries which are only vaguely like cut-work. Usually for these one of its more open varieties (Fig. 19 shows some very effective ones) is used in preference to the close stitch.

For example, the serviette ring in Fig. 47, except for the tiny stems and feather-stitched veins, is entirely in open buttonhole-stitch. This is worked round circularly for the little flowers, and after the ring and strap have been edged the surplus material outside these is cut away, as for scalloping.

In Fig. 48 all edges of the fascinating flower mats are carried out in long and short buttonhole-stitch (Fig. 19, *III*) before being cut away. Interior outlines are similarly worked, and only a few of the small markings are in outline stitches.

The advantage of buttonholing over mere outlining is that it

FIG. 48. The charm of buttonholed embroidery is seen in this flower luncheon set carried out in long-and-short buttonholing

not only enables the edges to be cut away in graceful shapes, but even in its more spaced varieties it has greater "body" and thickness than outline or chain stitchery.

Make a real friend of buttonhole-stitch. Learn to do it smoothly, strongly and evenly. It will help you with almost every type of embroidery there is, adding beauty, substance and colour.

7—(C.104)

USEFUL STITCHES FOR BUTTONHOLED AND CUT-WORK
EMBROIDERIES

Buttonhole-stitch itself is fully explained and illustrated in Chapter V. Here are some other stitches, not already given, which combine well with it.

FIG. 49. Seed-stitch—the back-stitched variety

Seed-stitch (Fig. 49). This is a quick and pretty filling stitch to give interest to a plain surface worked round with buttonhole-stitch. In elaborate cut-work it is used to fill flower petals.

Work small detached stroke- or back-stitches in various directions, scattering them fairly closely over the surface. Stroke-stitches give a comparatively flat effect, back-stitches a more raised appearance.

Triangular Feather-stitch (Fig. 83, right-hand stitch, page 155) is a decorative way of working the veins on cut-work or other leaves. It is useful, too, in building up borders, as described in Chapter III.

Use two imaginary parallel lines as guides. If working a leaf vein, these should run down each outside edge of the veining, with the "rib" of it lying midway between them. Working downwards, pick up a small stitch exactly along (say) the left-hand line. It should point towards you and the thread must be kept *under* the needle, as when working buttonhole-stitch—of which feather-stitch is a variation, really.

Pull up the thread, then take a second stitch, this time in the right-hand line, beginning level with the bottom of the first stitch. Again pull up the thread. Continue taking alternate stitches, each a little lower than the last, to each side.

Picots (Fig. 46, *D*) are pretty little loops which may be added, if liked, to the bars of Richelieu cut-work. Usually one is made midway along each bar, or picots may be worked at regular intervals round a buttonholed outer edge.

Work a picot as part of a bar. When buttonholing the bar, where the picot is to come do not pull a buttonhole-stitch quite tight, but leave enough of it loose to form a small loop, pinning this down to the material. Return by buttonholing over the doubled thread (Fig. 46, *E*), back to the bar, which is then continued.

Chapter X

WOOL EMBROIDERIES

NO wonder wool embroidery is so popular! It deserves to be, for its gaiety, its bold attractiveness and the quickness and ease with which it is worked. Beginners and little girls like it particularly for all these reasons, and even when you are an experienced and skilled embroideress you will give yourself a holiday sometimes by doing a piece of wool embroidery!

In the fancywork field, it corresponds to impressionism in art, getting its effects by splash and dash. Therefore, you must not expect elaborate detail or exquisite stitchery in this kind of work, but must get your results by broad treatment and quick, showy working.

You will see by this that wool embroideries are not really a separate type. In most cases very ordinary stitches and methods are used and simply adapted to the peculiar needs of wool, which, owing to its nature, demands a special—but very simple— technique.

One or two "wool only" kinds of embroidery are described in this chapter, and also some which can be worked in wool as well as in other threads. Tapestry, an important form of wool stitchery, is included with its near relation, cross-stitch, in Chapter XIII.

First, a few hints for wool embroideries in general, before dealing with each type separately.

Use wool needles (see page 3) as these, with their large eyes and rather blunt points, are specially fitted for this working thread. Always cut the wool. It is easily broken off, but to do so stretches it and results in ragged, frayed ends. Too small a needle also frays the wool. As wool gets ragged rather easily in any case, owing to its softness, use it in rather short lengths and discard it when it frays. Better to waste a little wool, you know, than to spoil the finished work!

Do not pull wool too tight or it goes thin and loses its beauty and elasticity. Stitches must not be really loose, of course, but they should not be the least bit dragged.

FIG. 50. Wool and silk threads form an effective alliance here in couching, lazy-daisy and underlaid buttonholing

Always use the simplest stitch that will give the effect wanted. Wool is so "blurry" that you will only get clear results by eliminating anything unnecessary. Rely on colour and line, not on elaborate stitchery. Outline and light filling stitches are better than solid satin-stitch, for instance, as in wool this easily looks heavy and uninteresting. For the same reason, use a spaced rather than a close buttonhole-stitch (see the good effect of the former on the felt puppy tea-cosy in Fig. 38).

FIG. 51. Dress embroidery, satin-stitched, in wool on wool

Stitches you will find specially useful in wool embroideries are: couching (page 43), French knots (page 27), running- or darning-stitch (page 55), back-stitch (page 55), lazy-daisy (page 26), outline-stitch (page 26), stroke-stitch (page 26), fly-stitch, and the filling stitch variously known as Roumanian or Cretan stitch. The last two are explained at the end of this chapter.

By the way, turn back to page 18, and note the effective use of darning, back-stitch and lazy-daisy wool stitches on linen in Fig. 5. At one time wool stitchery was used only on woollen fabrics, owing to the likelihood of its shrinking when laundered, but nowadays most embroidery wools are unshrinkable, and their rough texture may be used to give a pleasant contrast on such materials as crash, linen or sturdy cottons—or even on organdie (Fig. 54).

Speaking of contrast, this may also be obtained very prettily by blending the "hairiness" of woollen with the smooth shine of

Fig. 52. A "growing" design worked entirely in wool outline-stitch

silken threads. Fig. 50 shows this attractive alliance. Here the conventional flowers on a dressing-gown pocket are mainly couched, a very silky silk thread holding down the laid woollen one. Other details, such as tiny lazy-daisy loops round the flower edges, are

FIG. 53. Detail of wool embroidery on crash. It is mainly in Roumanian-stitch

also worked in silk. Along the pocket top the spaced buttonholing in silk is under-laid with woollen threads, as described on page 98.

This plan of mingling silk and wool stitchery is particularly pleasant for dress embroideries.

Wool Flower Embroidery

This uses simple flower designs well massed together (they are not effective if they straggle) and worked in some of the easy stitches already suggested. For dress purposes they may be

carried out on woollen material (see Fig. 51), but the effect is
usually better on a background of cotton (Fig. 52), linen or crash
(Fig. 53) or organdie (Fig. 54).

If cotton is selected, it must be loose enough in weave for

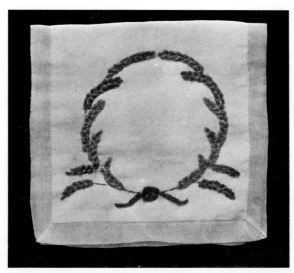

FIG. 54. This unusual handkerchief sachet has a chaplet of lavender
in wool satin-stitch

the rather large needle and thick thread to go through without
strain.

"Growing" designs, as in Fig. 52, where the tulips appear to
be actually pushing up from the soil, are particularly effective.

The stitches can hardly be too simple. In fact, the tulips in this
design are worked entirely in outline-stitch. Yet the effect is not
dull, because of the bright colours, shaded from light to dark on
both flowers and leaves, which are used.

When you look at the specimens in Figs. 51 and 54, you will
think that I have forgotten my statement, a page or two back, that
wool embroideries should not be worked in satin or solid filling

stitches. However, these are the exceptions that prove the rule, for in each case the design is so light and thin that it would look poverty-stricken if carried out only in outline stitches.

Rules are necessary to embroidery, as to most other things, but you will find a certain thrill in knowing just when and how to break them!

FIG. 55. What could be more effective and durable than Russian crash boldly couched in vivid rug wools?

RUG WOOL COUCHING

This bold fancy work is a little discovery of my own, made one day when I had a number of short oddments of rug wool, left from rug-making, which I wanted to use up.

This simplest and quickest of embroideries is splendid for large items which would take too long if decorated in slower ways. It gives most striking and vivid results for fire-screens, chair-backs, couch covers, wall panels, foot-stools and portières. Only one stitch, couching (see page 43), is used.

As the whole effect is coarse and bold, the background material should be chosen accordingly. Peasant crash is ideal and very cheap, while a heavy linen or cotton may also be used. A really *large* flowing design which can be worked in outline is needed; a good example is shown on the chair-back in Fig. 55.

Vivid colours—scarlet, royal blue, orange or emerald—look

best, especially on the drab surface of crash. Rug wool was used for the chair-back illustrated and is the best, perhaps, for the laid thread, but eight-ply wool is also good, especially if you want a rather softer and more subdued effect.

Thread a length of either wool into a rug needle. Bring it through to the right side somewhere on the design and couch it down with matching embroidery wool. If the needle is left hanging in the laid thread while it is being couched, it is then handy for taking the end of the thread back to the wrong side when the couching is finished. When the needle is too large to go through closely woven fabric, poke a hole for the rug wool with scissors.

One colour may be used throughout or the colours may vary in different parts of the design—green for leaves, brown for stems and so on. For a very bold outline couch round twice, putting the second line inside and touching the first.

Hems round the work should be finished with a couched line in the main colour used.

Wool Embroidery on Felt

This rather striking work does not take long to do, and is very effective for items which can be made in felt, such as cushion covers, pochettes, tea cosies (see the amusing one in Fig. 38) and luncheon table mats.

As felt does not fray and so can be used raw-edged without precautions being taken, it lends itself splendidly to appliqué, and most felt embroideries gain their colour and shape in this way. The embroidery is a secondary feature. On such a thick, dashing material as felt use the fewest and the boldest stitches possible. A very open buttonhole-stitch, as in Fig. 38, will hold the non-fray edges down to the background, while a few main outlines in the interior are soon worked in couching, lazy-daisy, back-stitch or French knots.

Stitchery may be in thick embroidery cotton, but it is best in embroidery wool. Do not attempt to match the wool to the appliqués. The effect is better if it is definitely lighter or darker, so as to relieve the large plain surfaces of the felt.

WOOL EMBROIDERY STITCHES

Some of the following stitches will be needed in the embroidery itself; others, such as fly-stitches, are very useful in working hems or simple borders round the embroidered articles.

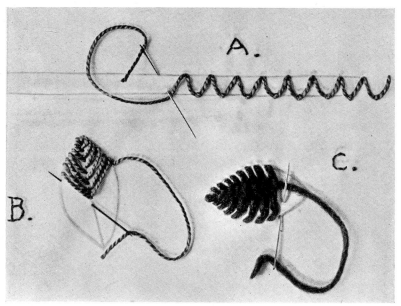

FIG. 56. *A*, fly-stitch; *B*, fishbone-stitch; *C*, Roumanian or Cretan-stitch

Remember that these stitches, though conveniently given here, are not confined to wool embroidery. Other uses for them are suggested under their separate headings.

Fly-stitch, for example, (Fig. 56, *A*) is very versatile. It will be a friend in need when building up the sort of designs suggested in Chapter III, for instance. Turn back to page 16, and you will see that it forms an important part of the border shown in Fig. **3**. Again, for the finishing of a right-side hem round a runner or other embroidered article, it is excellent, being decorative and speedily worked. It can also be used prettily as a simple trimming for children's clothes.

Actually this stitch is the open half of a lazy-daisy stitch. Fig. 56, *A*, shows its making clearly. Bring the needle through from the wrong side. On the same level, say $\frac{1}{4}$ in. farther to the left, insert it again in a slanting downward stitch, so that the point where it emerges forms a V with the two upper insertions. Keep the thread *under* the needle, as for the lazy-daisy stitch, and pull it up into a blunted V. Hold this down by taking a tiny bar across the point; then re-insert the needle at the second upper point to start the next V.

Y-stitch is a fly-stitch made with a long instead of a short bar, so that it has a tail or stem like the letter Y. It is a good, simple border stitch and is particularly effective on canvas, which makes it useful in the finishing of the edges of cross-stitched items.

Fish-bone Stitch (Fig. 56, *B*), is a useful, solid filling stitch for leaves. The stitches may be slightly separated (as in the illustration, where this is done for greater clearness) or worked so that they touch each other. If the leaf has no centre vein down it, mark one in pencil as a working guide.

Bring the needle through at the point of the leaf. Insert it the merest trifle beyond the centre line, on its left and far enough down to make the stitch a slanting one. Pull through, at the same time re-inserting the needle just to the left of the point. Continue to take a stitch from just the near side of the centre line to the right or left edge alternately until the leaf is filled.

Roumanian or Cretan-stitch (Fig. 56, *C*), is a picturesque filling stitch which covers well, but it is not quite so heavy or slow to work as satin-stitch. It is therefore particularly suited to large spaces or to wool embroidery. Note how gracefully it fills the flowers and leaves of the Spanish cushion in Fig. 99, of which Fig. 53 is an enlarged detail.

Work the stitch between two vertical lines or flower or leaf outlines. Bring the needle up on the right-hand line. Holding the thread down *under* the needle with the left thumb, take a short stitch to the right from the corresponding point on the left-hand line, as in the illustration, then a second short stitch to the left from a little lower down the right-hand line, and so continue alternating from side to side. According to the closeness of the filling wanted, work the stitches near enough to touch or with narrow spaces between.

Oriental Stitch (not illustrated) is a variation of Roumanian-stitch, suited for working leaf veins or fillings. Work it as a series of very shallow, outspread fly-stitches, with their bars touching each other all down the centre.

Underlaid Buttonhole-stitch quickly makes a wide colourful border or edging. It is used to finish the top edge of the pocket in Fig. 50. Start by working well-spaced buttonhole-stitch, prefer-ably in a strong or dark colour, over the edge, making deep "prongs" to it. Then run under the stitching, between it and the material, several lines of wool, each in a different shade.

Chapter XI

INITIALS AND LETTERING

I T is always nice to have a small piece of embroidery on hand, to do at odd moments or when sitting talking by the fire to your friends. Perhaps you have often thought how much it would add to the look of your house-linen if it were adorned with fine hand-worked initials. Well, why not take linen marking in this decorative way as your "odd times" embroidery, and get the lovely work done in moments that otherwise would probably be wasted?

Even if you cannot find the leisure to mark every piece with your monogram, try to do enough to furnish the guest room and bathroom beautifully. Start with your best pieces of linen, for it is hardly worth while to put good hand embroidery into inferior fabrics that will not wear very long. This is especially the case with large initials for such items as sheets.

Naturally if you are merely doing tiny monograms, very quickly worked, for dress items such as patch pockets, handkerchiefs and pochettes, the embroidery is soon done and it does not matter if its life is not a lengthy one.

The working of initials is not, in one sense, a special class of embroidery, for it varies so much in the style of letters and in the materials on which they are placed that you will find almost every stitch you know and every method you have tried are pressed into service at one time or another. This is part of the fascination of making monograms—the infinite variety that is possible.

On one side you are restricted—except for dress initials—and that is in colour. For some reason coloured initials on white household items seldom or never look well, and you will find it best for the initials to be all white. Tinted house linen, also, looks its best if embroidered in white or in exactly its own shade.

This lack of colour means that more attention is drawn to the

99

shapes of the letters and the stitchery used on them. So special care should be taken with both these points. Begin only with stitches you can do really well, choosing letters suited to them, and thoroughly practise any new stitches first on an oddment of the same material.

When selecting initials to embroider, choose them for their line, not for flourishing fancy touches. The latter are often used to disguise a poor shape or may merely muddle up a good one. And avoid like the plague initials or monograms which are so fantastic that nobody can tell at first glance what letters they really represent! The "A" in Fig. 57 is a little inclined to fall into this fault. Compare it with the simple dignity of the three-letter monogram in Fig. 58, or the decorative but clear "W" in Fig. 33, page 64, and you will see what I mean.

FIG. 57. This initial and shield have the outlines back-stitched, then filled with a thick line of couching. The bow is in satin-stitch

Plain initials are soon worked. If speed is your object, a good plan is to buy a felt or paper (the felt is better) "Reform" initial at a needlework shop.

It will cost 2d. or so, according to size, and is a cut-out initial. You merely place this in position on the linen and embroider over it with close, smooth satin-stitch. The initial is completely hidden, but gives a pleasing raised effect to the embroidery and obviates the need for a transfer. To add to its importance, if required, it may be outlined inside and out with back-stitch in a single strand of stranded cotton, worked in the same or a slightly darker shade.

For other initials transfers may be used. Plenty of variety, both in style and size, is obtainable in them. Or you can draw

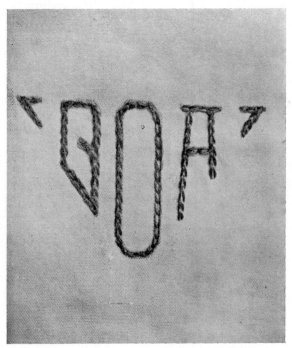

FIG. 58. Chain-stitch is quick and effective for slender initials

out yourself a plain straight letter such as an E or an H; if it seems to need a surround to set it off, cut a lozenge shape or circle out of paper, pin this over the initial outline and pencil round the edges. More elaborate shields, such as the circle and ribbon knot in Fig. 57, go with many transfers.

Still another simple plan is to cut out carefully the right letter from a newspaper or advertisement heading. Pin this in position on the material and pencil round it, afterwards back-stitching the pencilled outline. Enclose it in a surround, also back-stitched, and then fill all the space between the surround and the letter edges with one-way alternating darning (see page 65).   Unpin the letter and its shape will stand out clearly in plain material against the worked background.

The initial in Fig. 33 was worked by this easy and effective method. Note how the hem-stitched edge of the tray-cloth has been utilized to form two sides of the diamond surround—actually a square turned pointwise.

This is a comparatively slow method. Where you are using a monogram of two or three letters, yet want to work fast, an excellent plan is to use slender letters which can be filled lightly yet boldly with a single working of chain-stitch (Fig. 58). For a description of chain-stitch see the end of this chapter. In fact, this is one of the best and quickest monogram stitches, if not for the letters themselves, then often for all or part of any decoration, such as a true lovers' knot, surrounding them.

You will run no risk of forgetting your *broderie anglaise* when embroidering initials, for eyelets are extremely useful. Rather large letters are sometimes worked entirely in eyelets, slightly spaced out within the outlines; but they are really more effective when used sparingly here and there to give a light, openwork effect to heavy or much adorned initials.

On the other hand, very plain letters gain in charm if surrounded by a circle or oval consisting of spaced-out eyelets, as in Fig. 59. Such a surround also makes a small monogram look more imposing.

Another plan, very effective for hand towels, is to work the initials on a small triangle or circle of coloured cotton. Then blind-appliqué this to the towel, finally outlining the join with a very fine contrasting back-stitch.

LETTERING AND AUTOGRAPHS

Letters in embroidery are not always confined to mere initials. Sometimes whole words need to be worked, perhaps on a map, giving the names of places or of the country represented, as in Fig. 85, or often as an indication of the use of the embroidered

FIG. 59. This rather enlarged photograph shows the good effect of eyelets encircling a plain monogram

item or its contents, as in the case of "Pyjamas" on a bed sachet or "Whisk Broom" on the little holder in Fig. 60.

With two or three words to embroider, naturally the fairly

elaborate methods used for initials are too slow and rather unsuitable. Words, if large, as when giving the name of the contents or the title of a map or book cover, must be carried out boldly yet simply. Some of the best stitches to use are running-stitch (Fig. 60), outline-stitch, back-stitch and chain-stitch. To give a more solid effect with little extra work, a word in a dark shade in outline-stitch may be "lined" with a second row in a lighter colour, or *vice versa.*

Turn to Fig. 85, page 160, where the word "California," which must not be too light and thin because of the rather heavy border surrounding it, is so embroidered. Effective, isn't it?

For small, fine lettering, such as autographs, or the names of towns on a map, use a fine thread and keep to either outline- or split-stitch (page 26). Verses on samplers are invariably worked in fine cross-stitch (see Chapter XIII).

FIG. 60. Running stitch is good for embroidering simple wording

Perhaps you will say, after reading the above paragraph, "Autographs? When does one work autographs?" for it seldom seems to occur to needleworkers to embroider names. Yet it is such a simple, quick plan, if you want to mark, say, a handkerchief as your property, to write your name small across one corner with a pencil and then work over it with a single strand of stranded cotton.

Teach this simple trick to schoolgirls and they will save

you the bother of marking their handkerchiefs and underwear for them! Use a boil-proof thread, of course.

Again, why not copy great-grandmamma, who used to collect all her friends' signatures, written large and bold with a soft pencil,

FIG. 61. One corner of an interesting autographed table-cloth, with border worked in link darning

on a home-made linen tea-cloth? She worked over the autographs in outline-stitch, taking care to preserve their individuality, made a pleasant border round the cloth, and there was a permanent yet usable record of the friendships of years!

A pretty idea, isn't it? Modern embroideresses are copying this notion, which is now old enough to be new, and Fig. 61 shows an up-to-date version. A simple border (described on page 66) holds down the hem and each corner is dedicated to signatures, arranged haphazard as the writers pleased. The cloth belongs to a girl who started it during her engagement, allotting one corner to her family and friends, another to her fiancé's family and friends, a third to people associated with the engagement period and the wedding, and the fourth to new friends made after marriage.

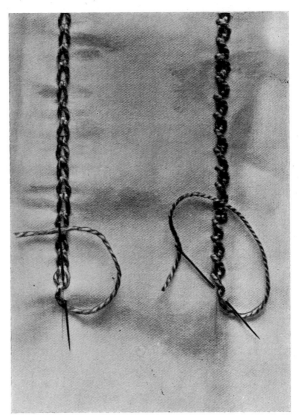

FIG. 62. *Left*, chain-stitch; *Right*, twisted chain-stitch

I myself have completed a similar cloth, but with the signatures arranged in a wide band inside a coloured border, in order to keep the centre clear for use. It is filled with the autographs of friends whom I have entertained in my own home. You must have some little condition of this sort, or the cloth becomes a mere collection of names that stand for nothing!

Naturally, such cloths as these two need years to complete and make nice pick-up work to do occasionally. But if you start one (or a tray-cloth) for people met on a particular holiday—say a cruise—it will not take long to finish.

USEFUL STITCHES FOR INITIALS AND LETTERING

Chain-stitch (Fig. 62, left-hand stitch) has a dozen different uses, which are noted in this book as they occur. It is a real embroidery maid-of-all-work, for it has many uses and is also an excellent padding stitch, filling in a single working as efficiently as several lines of running-stitch.

To work the stitch, bring the needle through at the top of a line or design, and work downwards or towards yourself. This is one of the loop stitches, so the thread must be kept always under the needle. Put the needle in close to where it emerged, holding down the thread to form a loop. Pull up the thread a trifle slackly. Insert the needle in the loop, near its base, bring it out a little lower down and so form the second loop. Continue similarly, always starting just inside the previous loop and holding the thread down under the needle.

The effect, as you see, greatly resembles the links of a chain.

Twisted Chain-stitch (Fig. 62, right-hand stitch) is an ornamental variation of chain-stitch giving a more broken and imposing effect. It is excellent for straight, rather plain initials when you want to make them look a little more "fancy," as a decorative hem round embroidered items, or as a simple dress trimming.

Work as for chain-stitch, except that when starting each stitch (except the first one) do not place it inside the previous loop, but slantwise across the line being worked, as in the illustration. That is to say, you are working your chain with each link slanted or twisted instead of vertical, though the stitch as a whole forms a vertical line.

Ladder or Roman-stitch (Fig. 63) is another member of the large loop-stitch family. It forms a quick and pretty way, light in effect, of working simple initials. It is a good stitch to use when building up decorative borders, and a charming way of adding lace prettily to underwear or household linens.

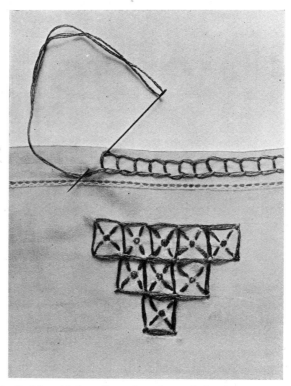

FIG. 63. Ladder-stitch. *Above*, how to work it; *Below*, a decorative motif built up in this stitch

It is really a buttonhole-stitch. Work it as for spaced buttonhole-stitch (page 42) with a dash of chain-stitch thrown in! To be more precise, work spaced buttonhole-stitch but with the needle *slanting forward* instead of upright to form each stitch, and with that same stitch starting from inside the previous loop. This apparently gives a triangle and looks wrong when compared with the finished square stitch. But draw up the thread rather slackly, and when the next slanting stitch is taken inside it the triangle is automatically pulled out into a square.

Fig. 63 also shows ladder-stitch formed into a simple motif, by three diminishing rows being first built up and then each square being filled with a run-in multiplication sign that has a French knot in its open centre.

When using this stitch to join on lace, tack the lace to the right side of the material, overlapping it by $\frac{1}{2}$ in. Work the ladder-stitch over the join, taking the top of each stitch through both lace and material, and the bottom of each stitch through the stuff only, a trifle below the lace.

Chapter XII

HEM-STITCHING AND DRAWN-THREAD WORK

EMBROIDERIES which are based on drawing threads one way of the fabric, and working the threads that remain into patterns and borders by means of embroidery stitches, vary very widely in their type and in the stitches they use. Accordingly, it seems best in this chapter to depart from my usual practice of grouping all stitches together at the end of the chapter and to describe them as they occur under each heading.

Drawn-thread embroideries, like *broderie anglaise* and cut-work, depend for their beauty on the contrast of a dark space or background, showing through where the threads are drawn, with the pale solidity of the material used. So they look their best when used against dark surfaces, as when made into sideboard and table runners, table-cloths, luncheon-table mats and duchesse sets. They wash excellently.

For these two reasons they are often combined with *broderie anglaise*, as already mentioned, a drawn-thread stitch forming a hem for such work.

Drawn-in drawn-thread work and needle weaving only are exceptions to these remarks, for here the spaces left by drawing threads are filled in with new ones of a different colour.

Remember that two conditions are necessary for any form of drawn-thread work and choose your material and design accordingly. These conditions are—

1. The material must have such a weave that threads may be pulled out easily. Linen is the fabric that instantly comes to mind, but voile, shantung silk and many modern loosely-woven woollens are just as suitable. With a little more patience, too, the threads may be drawn from many soft cottons.

2. All hems or patterns must be straight-line ones, because they follow the weave. It is impossible to do drawn-thread work

on curves or slants. For these latter mock hem-stitching, known as faggoting or veining (see Chapter XIV), is the nearest substitute.

Hem-stitching

This is not a class of embroidery, but merely a numerous group of drawn-thread stitches which are used in many kinds of fancy work. As their name suggests, their chief use is to finish hems in a decorative and transparent way, and you will find yourself continually using one or other of them to "set off" such varying types of embroidery as inlay (Fig. 18), darning (Figs. 28 and 33), *broderie anglaise* (Figs. 36 and 37), monogram stitchery (Fig. 59) and cross-stitch (Fig. 70), not to mention various foreign embroideries described in Chapter XVII.

In fact, you will find so many uses for hem-stitching that it is worth your while to know half a dozen different varieties. Home needlewomen are too apt to get into a rut of using always simple and bar hem-stitching, and these only; whereas it is easy and interesting to ring the changes to suit your particular piece of work. To help you in this, I am giving here a number of really interesting hem-stitches, some from abroad and very little known in England. I have picked out those which, besides being pretty and unhackneyed, are easy to learn and fairly quick to do.

Though the first use of hem-stitching is for hems, it does not depend in any way on there being a fold of material, and it is often worked on the flat surface to form interior panels or to divide, say, a cloth into squares. In Fig. 70, page 128, two lines of it (only one is shown) are used to form a border round the cloth on which the cross-stitch pattern is worked.

It is also much used as a simple dress decoration of rather severe type on sports frocks and underwear, when these are of suitable materials and shapes. It may edge a "best" handkerchief or border the square neck, patch pockets and belt of a washable dress.

Six out of the first seven hem-stitches described below are illustrated in the hem-stitched sampler (Fig. 64) on page 113.

For any hem-stitch begin, where the stitch is to come, by pulling out a number of threads next to each other to form a "run." This run should be $\frac{1}{8}$ in. or $\frac{3}{16}$ in. wide, as a rule, but naturally varies according to the weave and the size of what you are making. If it is a hem you are doing, crease and tack it so that its inner fold comes just to the beginning of the run.

When pulling out threads which do not go from end to end of the stuff (as when marking out squares or panels), to keep them from drawing out too far mark each end of the run with a pin and then cut the thread at these points before starting to withdraw it.

Simple Hem-stitch (Fig. 64, top stitch, to the left of the needle). Work on the wrong side from left to right, preferably holding your work with the hem or its bottom edge downwards or towards yourself. For this and for all the following hem-stitches, unless otherwise stated, use matching sewing cotton or a *fine* embroidery thread, as the thread should show as little as possible.

Secure the thread in the hem or firm part of the stuff and bring the needle through close to the run. Take up four vertical threads (called strands) in the run; then insert the needle again diagonally behind the four strands as in the illustration, emerging in the edge of the hem. Pull the thread tightly round the strands and make a little stitch into the hem fold or into the solid edge when there is no hem. This keeps the pulled threads firmly together. Put the needle behind the next four strands and repeat.

You will understand that four strands is an average number to take up, but naturally the size of the groups varies according to the weave. So use your own judgment whether to take up three, four, five or even six strands, not only in this but in the other hem-stitches given.

Double or Bar Hem-stitch (Fig. 64, top row, to the *right* of the needle). This is merely simple hem-stitch worked twice, once along each edge of the run. The groups of strands, instead of forming triangles as in the simple variety, become narrow bars with large spaces between.

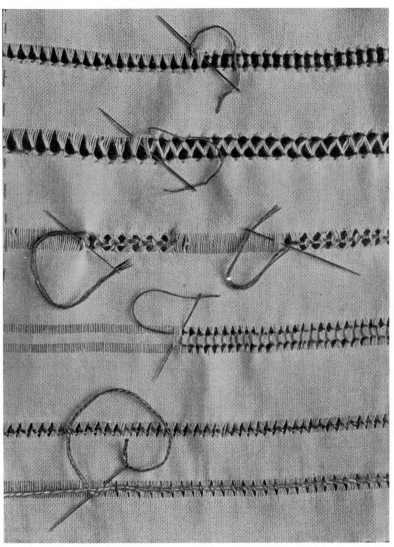

FIG. 64. A sampler of hem-stitches, showing:
Top line, simple hem-stitch (*left*), bar hem-stitch (*right*)
Second line, diagonal hem-stitch
Third line, single crossing (two stages)
Fourth line, Italian hem-stitch
Fifth line, two-way hem-stitch (*right side*)
Sixth line, two-way hem-stitch (*wrong side*)

This is perhaps the commonest of all hem-stitches. Notice its use in Fig. 59, where it is shown somewhat enlarged.

Diagonal Hem-stitch, though it looks so different from bar hem-stitch (you see it in Fig. 64, second line down), is only slightly different. To get the pretty zigzag effect, proceed as for bar hem-stitch, but when working along the second edge take up half the strands of one group and half of another together, as illustrated, instead of working group by group. Make your run $\frac{3}{16}$ in. to $\frac{1}{2}$ in. wide.

This stitch is used for the hem of the towel in Fig. 67.

Alternate Hem-stitch (not illustrated) is another bar variation, giving an effective series of triangles, alternately each way up. Work as for bar hem-stitch, but after taking up and tightening the first group of strands, take a stitch along the edge (with the thread on the wrong side, just into the firm part) so as to pass behind and miss the next group. Continue thus hem-stitching every other group all along. Then work the second line, this time taking up only the groups left before. Pull the thread round the strands really tightly to define the triangles well. Sewing cotton is the best to use.

Single Crossing (Fig. 64, third row from top) is a charming twisted hem-stitch, quite original in effect. It needs only a single line of stitchery through the centre of the run. Secure the thread, and then pass the needle over the first four strands, but pick up the next four with a *backward* stitch (with the needle pointing towards the start of the work, not forward), as shown by the right-hand needle. Still holding these four strands on the needle, twist it backwards under the whole eight strands to give a crossed or plaited effect (left-hand needle). Pull the thread taut through the twisted part, and repeat the whole stitch with the next eight strands.

Italian or Square Hem-stitch (Fig. 64, fourth row from top), is worked on a double run, and with embroidery thread contrasting with the material to give a colour effect. So it is rather an imposing stitch, as the illustration shows, and yet one which is very quickly worked. One or two lines of it make a pretty decoration along the top of a modesty vest or it is a striking hem for embroidered articles.

Make the run by drawing one thread (close up to the hem if there is one), leaving four threads, and then drawing one more. In the illustration, for greater clearness, three threads were drawn on each run and six left between them, giving a wider and more open effect, but the one-and-four arrangement is the usual one.

Work towards yourself. After securing the thread, take a forward stitch along one run, picking up four or five threads; then back-stitch back over those threads. Carry the thread straight (not slanting, as seems more natural) across the solid ground between the runs on the right side. Take forward and back-stitch here again into the second run, picking up the same number of stitches. Then take the thread back again to the first run, but this time take it on the *wrong* side and in a forward slant (see the needle in the illustration), so as to be in position to make the back-stitch on this side. Go on repeating from there.

Briefly put, draw together a group of strands on one run, cross straight on the right side, draw together the matching group on the second run, and cross again in a slanting direction on the wrong side.

Two-way or Couched Hem-stitch. This is an idea of my own. It is perhaps the quickest of all hem-stitches, gives contrasting colour effects and is equally pretty (though different) on the two sides, which makes it useful for a handkerchief or scarf. It is not really a hem finish, merely a decorative line. In Fig. 64, the fifth line from the top shows the right side, and the bottom line illustrates the wrong-side effect.

Work on the wrong side. Lay a rather thick embroidery thread down the middle of the run, and couch it down by making bar stitches over it at intervals, each stitch taking up the same number of strands. The couching thread should contrast with the laid thread.

Overcast Hem-stitch. This is clearly seen in Figs. 36 and 37 (pages 69 and 70) where it borders the *broderie anglaise* breakfast set. Use a narrow run about five threads wide, close to the hem. This is a hem finish only and cannot be used for lines of decoration away from an edge.

Tack a narrow hem—say $\frac{3}{8}$ in. wide—and at its inner fold draw a run $\frac{1}{8}$ in. wide. Use a fairly thick embroidery cotton which contrasts with the material in colour.

Make two upright overcasting stitches side by side over the hem, putting the second one into the run through the loop of the first. Now take a running-stitch $\frac{1}{4}$ in. long over the run, letting the stitch lie a little loose, and then a shorter back-stitch immediately beyond this. Pull the back-stitch tight. Repeat all along, overcasting twice, running once and back-stitching once. The effect is most decorative.

Herringbone Hem-stitch (a glimpse of it is shown in Fig. 70) makes a wide, rather imposing double hem-stitch for edging borders or panels. It is most successful on a soft cotton or silk, not on a firm, round-thread linen, as it has not a tight pull to separate tough strands firmly. Work with matching sewing cotton. Draw two runs, with a wider undrawn band between them—say four threads for the runs and six for the centre band.

Now work herringbone-stitch (see page 153) along the undrawn portion, with each stitch taking up a group of threads first in one run and then in the other. Pull up the stitches taut, but not tight enough to pucker the undrawn band.

A slower but better way of working this stitch results in both sides being exactly alike. In this case, make the runs wider than the centre part. On the right side first herringbone across the centre band into each run in turn, slanting the stitches well so as to leave alternate groups of strands in each run unworked. Then return on the wrong side, and herringbone-stitch these unworked groups.

Diamond Hem-stitch differs from the others in being all-over, so that you can make it in square, oblong or triangular panels to adorn dress or household items. Fig. 65 shows it on a night-dress case of linen. Tweedy materials also take it well if they are firm. It is apt to pucker a soft, loosely woven fabric.

Mark out the panel as explained on page 112, and then draw runs both ways of the stuff to form open checks. The runs can be

Fig. 65. A panel of handsome diamond hem-stitch is the sole trimming on a linen night-dress case

any width you like, but you must always draw only half as many threads as are left between two runs. A proportion of six drawn threads to twelve undrawn ones suits most fabrics.

First work a small spaced buttonhole-stitch, in matching sewing cotton, all round the panel edge. Then go up and down the rows of threads (bars) left between the runs, on the *wrong* side, working a single buttonhole-stitch over each little bar, up one row and down the next. Afterwards repeat on the crosswise rows. Each stitch pulls the previous one tight, narrowing the bars into the diamond shown in Fig. 65.

If both sides are to look equally neat, as for scarf ends, work the hem-stitch differently, after preparing and buttonholing the edges in the same way. From the right side whip over each bar twice, the second time catching up the first whipping thread so that it is centred neatly. Whip every row both vertically and horizontally, always pulling the thread very tight.

You will like this handsome hem-stitch for decorating cushion covers, chair-backs, runners and table-cloths, as well as dress items.

Drawn-in Drawn-thread Work

This is also called American weaving, as it originated in the United States. Really it is only by courtesy that it is included in an embroidery book, for no needle is used for making it, but it is so often allied with embroidery, as on the tray-cloth in Fig. 66, that no book on hand stitchery is quite complete without it.

Whoever invented this process (one cannot call it a stitch) was little short of a genius! For by the simplest and quickest method ever heard of one can insert a coloured line or lines into a fabric as perfectly as if it were woven in by machine.

It is best suited to comparatively fine materials, particularly voile, shantung silk and handkerchief linen. If fast colours are used the inserted thread washes as well and wears as long as the material into which it is drawn. The best thread to use is stranded cotton, as this can be so easily suited to the weave by using the right number of strands. One strand only is needed for the fine materials already mentioned.

Remember that this trimming is very difficult to do in long lines, owing to breakage of threads. I once succeeded in decorating all round the top of a pair of cami-knickers with it, but that was a difficult, tedious job which I do not recommend you to copy. If you limit yourself to lines not more than 15 in. long, you will still be able to use this type of work for tray-cloths, runners (across the ends), luncheon-table mats, table centres, modesty vests and patch

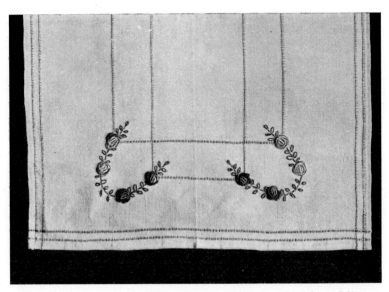

FIG. 66. Part of a tray-cloth adorned with drawn-in coloured lines
and bullion-stitch roses

pockets. It is particularly successful on linen handkerchiefs, as both sides are exactly alike.

To draw in a coloured line, completely pull out one thread of material where the line is to come. If it goes only partly across the stuff, like the short lines stopped by the embroidery in Fig. 66, cut the thread at each end before drawing it.

Just start to pull out the next thread to it, but stop when you have freed one end of it an inch or two. Tie this end to the loop of a strand of stranded cotton, cut a little more than twice the length of the thread pulled out, and doubled in half. Now finish drawing completely out the tied-on thread, but *from the other end.* As it emerges it will draw after it, into precisely the position it occupied, the doubled coloured thread attached to it, giving an illusion of perfect weaving.

Everything depends, of course, on the pulled-out second thread not breaking, but coming out in one piece. To make sure of this pull slowly and gently, and every inch or two change your grip, so that the strain comes constantly on a different part of the thread.

You will soon get the knack of pulling the thread out whole, if you start with short lines and work up gradually to longer ones. Should an occasional accident happen, pull the broken thread right out, tie the coloured strand to the next thread and try again. The only drawback will be that the coloured strand will be a little loose in the fabric.

When a coloured line is in position, cut off any surplus flush with the material edges or with the end of the line.

Simple as the work is, you can get great variety into it by varying the number of lines, their colour, length and distance apart. Two or three lines set close together, the outermost close up to the inner fold of a hem, make an effective border.

The work is usually prettiest if combined with some simple outline embroidery, such as the sprays of bullion-stitched rosebuds in Fig. 66. Short lines or the right-angles of interlaced squares may be finished with little flowers consisting of three or four lazy-daisy stitches or with clusters of rainbow-hued French knots.

NEEDLE-WEAVING OR SWEDISH DARNING

Though a form of darning, as its alternative name implies, this bold and brilliant embroidery is included under drawn-thread work because it is darned over runs in the material. It is perhaps the most dashing of all embroideries, and has much more vivid colouring than most drawn-thread work.

You will find it a striking embellishment for such things as chair-backs, linen towels (Fig. 67), cushion covers and runners.

The original needle-weaving from Sweden concentrated on these comparatively large things, and was carried out with thick threads on coarse materials. But if you have plenty of patience and good eyes, you can use it as a most beautiful way of adorning your own

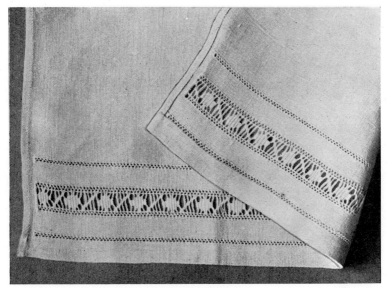

FIG. 67. Towel with needle-woven border, practically the same on both sides

voile blouses (see the example in Fig. 68) and little frocks for children made of the same material.

Swedish darning has the advantage over other forms of drawn-thread work that it does not weaken the fabric, but firmly welds the runs together. Crash, hessian, linen and coarse jute fabrics are all suitable for the work. On coarse weaves use a thick thread such as Flox, Artello Twist, or No. 3 Star Sylko.

The work is done as borders, bands or panels. If you are making your first attempt at this work, start with a narrow border, as the wide bands, though handsomer, take more practice to work well. A neutral-coloured material needle-woven in brilliant colours generally gives the best result.

Patterns are of a geometrical type and built up on the run as you go along; or they can be copied by counting from a book of needle-weaving designs. When you are familiar with the work you will find it easy and fascinating to make up your own designs, working them out first on squared paper unless they are very simple.

The easiest border of all to work is one consisting only of darned bars (the shorter and lower line in Fig. 69). This gives a very open effect, and may either form a simple decoration by itself, if made rather wide, or when narrow may be worked above and below a more elaborate one, to give the latter a finish.

If the line of decoration is to stand alone, draw a run $\frac{1}{2}$ in. to $\frac{3}{4}$ in. wide. Should this not extend across the entire width of the material, cut the threads before pulling (see page 112) and button-hole the cut edges to keep them from fraying. I personally like a finer thread for buttonholing than that used for the weaving.

Secure the thread at one end with a back-stitch or two, avoiding a knot. The threads are worked in groups of three, four or what-ever number suits the weave of the fabric; each group is called a set or block. Leave about an inch width at one end unworked.

Two blocks or sets are darned into one bar. (This form of bar may also be used in cut-work, by the way.) Darn over the first set and under the second, starting at the top of the run. Then return by reversing the darning, i.e. over the second block and under the first. Continue darning to and fro in this way, which makes the stitches interlace neatly between the two sets, all down the run. Then darn the next two sets in the same way.

The darning will pull the sets together considerably, leaving quite wide spaces between the finished bars. If liked, you can use two colours, alternating them for each bar; or a beautiful result is gained by shading, in tones, say, from cream through yellow and orange to brown, either by using a rainbow (shaded) thread or by changing the colour every bar or two to a thread one tone deeper.

After working bars you will want to try a more ambitious pattern. Such patterns often run diagonally, so that it may be necessary to work half of one bar, and then continue that colour

FIG. 68. Needle-woven panel on a voile blouse

by darning the second set of the first bar together with a new bar, and half-way down that to begin on sets three and four. See the upper right-angle band in Fig. 69. Do not, however, get too far across from the starting point with one colour before changing to another and working the intervening sets.

Remember that all darning must be close enough to hide the strands of the run entirely. When working running patterns do not draw the darning so tight as with bars; there must be spaces between one bar and the next but they should not be wide ones—more like slits, in fact. Exceptions to this are when both material and working are in one colour (see Fig. 67) when the contrast of large spaces to the monochrome effect is needed, and in very soft materials such as voile (Fig. 68) which pull together owing to their thinness however loosely you darn.

Finishing Corners. When you darn a border all round a square or oblong of fabric, as for a runner, the withdrawing of threads both ways will leave a square hole in each corner. This must be filled with an ornamental motif of some kind, in a way rather similar to the filling of cut-work spaces with bars.

First prepare the empty square by closely buttonholing its edges all round. If the material frays and stretches easily, as needle-weaving fabrics often do, put in a line of running-stitches slightly inside the edges before buttonholing.

The Cobweb Corner, shown in Fig. 69, is pretty and easy to work. To make the "spokes" of the web, lay single threads across as follows.

Start with a knot at the inner corner, go across to the middle of the upper side, and then along the wrong side through the button-holing to the outer corner. Take the thread diagonally back from there to the inner corner where you started, then outwards to the middle of the lower or vertical side. From here go through the buttonholing on the wrong side to the corner horizontally level with the inner starting corner. Finally, take the thread back to the inner corner over the last thread of strand of material, and then similarly along the fourth side to the upper left-hand corner. Here take the thread through to the wrong side and fasten off.

With a fresh thread darn over and under the five spokes, alternating back and forth until they are half-filled, as in Fig. 69.

The corner should be worked before the weaving of the pattern reaches right up to it; then you can "anchor" the sides of the corner securely by taking one weaving stitch each side (when finishing your weaving) into the darning.

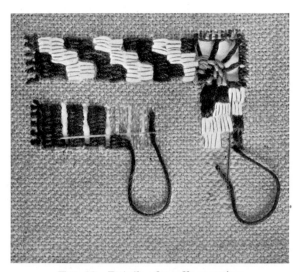

FIG. 69. Details of needle-weaving
Top and vertically downwards on right, a diagonal two-colour pattern with a cobweb corner
Below, woven bars

Needle-weaving is not very easy to do well. Before leaving the subject, here are some special hints to help you.

1. Starting or fastening off new threads is tricky, as they easily disarrange the weaving if drawn through the back of it to secure them. When possible, knot the new thread on to the old one. Be very careful when working not to put the thread through a previous stitch, catching or splitting it.

2. When working a pattern which runs diagonally (as in Fig. 69, upper border) you may need at the start and finish to work only a single set (instead of an entire bar) here and there, in a

particular colour. These cannot be darned—just wrap them. The pattern shown is in only two colours, but three, four or even five are often used. It is easiest to have each colour on a separate needle.

3. If the threads of material (strands) are finer one way of the weave than the other, you may need to vary the number of threads in a set to keep the bars the same width.

4. Instead of buttonholing the cut edges of a panel to prevent fraying, a very neat plan is to cut the threads to be drawn in the middle of their length, instead of at each end. Then darn every alternate thread invisibly back into the uncut part of the material, cutting off the intermediate threads just flush with the panel ends.

Chapter XIII

CROSS-STITCH AND TAPESTRY

IF you find stitches difficult to remember and yet like variety in the embroidery itself, you will take to cross-stitch fancy work as to the manner born! For this, like cut-work, is a one-stitch embroidery—and that one stitch so simple that no one could possibly forget it! Yet, elementary as it is, it can be used for so many different types of work that you will never complain of monotony.

Except when cross-stitch is done by the counting method on canvas, no thought or effort is required at all, and so it is ideal stitchery for the "tired business girl" or for that naughty creature (yes, she does exist!) who likes to sew and read at the same time.

The actual cross-stitch is described at the end of this chapter. Here let us say something about the many interesting ways in which it is used.

Cross-stitch has a long history and in bygone times it was always worked on material with countable threads, such as linen or canvas—witness the old samplers which we treasure as antiques to-day. (See Fig. 90, page 173.) Patterns and designs could be bought, printed out in colours on paper wth a tiny check; if you still have great-grandmother's work-box among your family possessions, you will probably find in it a booklet of such cross-stitch copies.

But the close counting and copying made the work tedious and some of the material used, being finely woven, must have imposed a great strain on the eyes—especially in those days of lamps and candles. So nowadays we nearly always do the job much more quickly and easily by using transfers, on which every cross-stitch is clearly marked. This is the best method in nine cases out of every ten.

It may happen, though, that you want to copy a pattern for

127

which no transfer is available. You can then use the counting method if your fabric is of a large weave, such as crash or canvas,

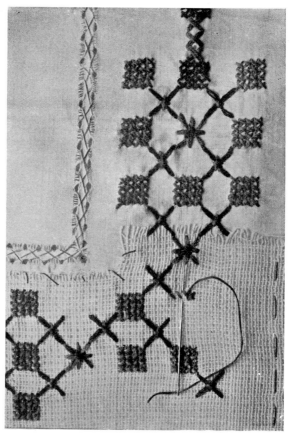

FIG. 70. Cross-stitch design being worked on to a fine fabric through canvas, also a glimpse of herringbone hem-stitch

but if it is really finely woven, so that counting is impossible, what are you to do then?

Fig. 70 supplies the simple answer. Buy enough cross-stitch

Fig. 71. An attractive breakfast-set in shaded cross-stitch

canvas to take the design, tack this securely over your material and then copy the pattern by counting the canvas, making all stitches, of course, through both canvas and the material beneath. It is necessary to work rather tightly, so that the stitches will not be loose in the finished work.

When the embroidery is complete, pull out the canvas one thread at a time, and the design remains correctly worked on your material.

There is just one snag, and the first time I tried this method I struck it and received a horrid shock. The canvas was stiff and strong and resolutely refused to pull out! Not a thread could I budge! If your canvas is this unaccommodating kind, remember that it is stiffened with size or glue, and soak it to make it pliable. I had to do this after the embroidery was finished, which is a bad plan. You will be able to profit by my experience and test a little of the canvas, before tacking it in place, to see whether soaking is required. If it is, use warm water, and when the canvas is soft after immersion be careful that you do not pull the squares out of shape.

The threads now not only pull out readily when required, but the softness of the canvas allows you to work it quickly, whereas when stiff the needle must be stabbed in it to and fro.

Note, by the way, in Fig. 70, the good and quick results obtained by varying the blocks of small crosses, which are comparatively slow to work, with larger cross-stitches that give a pleasing open effect. As these stitches are long enough to catch in things, they are held down where they cross with a tiny cross-stitch to each. An occasional star, made by working an upright cross (thus +) over a multiplication sign (thus ×) is also used to give variety.

This particular pattern is worked in a thick mercerised embroidery cotton, but cross-stitch has as many possible threads as it has methods and types, and the photographs illustrating this chapter show it also worked in a finer cotton thread (Fig. 71) and in wool (Fig. 72). Rugs are sometimes cross-stitched in rug wool or a very thick jute yarn.

Cross-stitchery is generally most effective in bright colours on a white or neutral ground, because, like most simple stitchery, it

FIG. 72. Collar and cuffs worked in solid wool cross-stitch in contrasting colours

depends largely on colour contrast. Sometimes pastel tones are used and shading is carried out (Fig. 71), but unless colours and design are skilfully chosen the result always seems to me rather timid and uninteresting. A notable exception is where the design is not straggling, but in fairly solid masses, when it can be wonderfully enhanced by the cross-stitch shapes being outlined all round with a fine black or dark back-stitch.

Most often, as the photographs show you, the design has a background of plain material, a worked background being more

FIG. 73. In Assisi embroidery the design is outlined in back-stitch and the background cross-stitched

usual in tapestry than in cross-stitch. But when you are only working small areas, such as a jumper collar or a serviette ring, a very striking result is soon obtained by cross-stitching both the design and the background (on canvas) in sharply contrasting colours. See the collar and cuffs in Fig. 72. They are worked in embroidery wool.

Cross-stitch combines well with outline embroidery, as in Fig. 9.

ASSISI WORK

This is a very effective form of cross-stitch dating from the Middle Ages. It came from Italy, gaining its name from the town of Assisi (associated with the great St. Francis) in that country.

The original designs used dated centuries back and were mostly of imaginary birds and dragons such as were believed in centuries ago. It is nice, if possible, to preserve the character of this embroidery by using transfers of a similar kind, and they also make a change from floral designs, but, if you cannot obtain them, transfers of modern type, so long as they are flowing and well broken up, give just as pretty results.

As Fig. 73 shows you, in Assisi work the usual plan is reversed and the background is cross-stitched, so that the design is thrown up boldly against it in white, or whatever is the shade of the material used.

If possible, choose a white or light natural material and work the cross-stitch background all in one rich colour. For clear definition the unworked design is outlined, after the cross-stitching is done, with back-stitch made as a double running-stitch (see page 56). Black or a very dark shade is best for this outlining, which some people, by the way, prefer to do first of all.

TAPESTRY OR PETIT POINT

This has come back into favour remarkably during the last few years. It has various names, such as tapestry, *petit point* (French, little stitch) and needlepoint. The point of the last two is difficult to see! Even the name "tapestry" is rather misleading, for this is, of course, properly a woven fabric. However needle-point is called by the woven fabric's name after the famous Bayeux tapestries, which were embroidered in *petit point*.

You get a clear idea of tapestry if you think of it as a quicker form of cross-stitch, carried out in heavier canvas and wools so that it is suitable for furnishing purposes. If you want to do a piece of work which your descendants will treasure as an heirloom, needlepoint gives you your chance, for several lifetimes will hardly suffice to wear it out.

As it is used for rather large things, such as the chair seat in Fig. 74, foot-stool and cushion covers, fire-screens and even rugs, and you have to work the entire fabric, background as well as design, it is naturally not a quick form of embroidery. So never try to do it in a hurry—except, perhaps, a little handbag in finer *petit point*.

FIG. 74. This fine old chair has a hand-made *petit point* cover in charming patchwork effect

A much better plan is to spend months or even years over a piece of tapestry, working on it for an hour or a day just whenever you feel inclined or have no more speedy embroidery in hand. As a stand-by of this sort, requiring no brain fag to execute, it is fascinating work, and the finished product will beautify your home for many years after you have forgotten the time spent in making it.

Practically without exception, it is worked in wools on canvas. Occasionally a handbag may be done in silk, and Victorian workers often mingled beads or touches of silk with their wool work; but only wool is hard-wearing enough for chair and foot-stool covers, at least. Buy the special large-meshed Penelope canvas sold for tapestry. Special tapestry wools are also sold, but are not essential. The delightful modern patchwork chair cover in Fig. 74, for instance, was carried out in ordinary embroidery wool used double, as you will see by the detail illustration, Fig. 75.

For the most usual tapestry stitch, called tent-stitch, and for others not quite so well known, see pages 139–40.

Old tapestry, like old cross-stitch, was copied from a chart and counted out stitch by stitch on plain canvas. As Fig. 75 shows, the modern diamond design was worked in the same way, a medley of many colours being used in a hit-or-miss fashion to give a patchwork effect. If you are copying this design, as you can easily do from the detail illustration, remember that the most amazing variety of colours will blend in well together, owing to the black diamond framework which holds them all together harmoniously. This is a very gay idea for using up oddments of wool.

Decide first on about three main colours and buy $\frac{1}{4}$ lb. of each of these. Then add to them all the oddments of the right kind of wool which you have left over from knitting or embroidery and buy small skeins or balls of a dozen other colours not already in your collection. Always work the black framework and crosses first, before filling in the diamonds. The black centre dot in each diamond is a cross-stitch; otherwise the whole cover is in tent stitch. Work the centres of the black crosses (not yet filled in in Fig. 75) all in the same neutral shade—beige or grey.

Remember when doing any tapestry that it is not washable, so that it should not contain much light colour that will soil quickly.

If you do not care for copying a design in this way, at slightly more expense you can buy a sheet of canvas ready stencilled in the correct colour with an attractive design. You have then only to go over each canvas square with a stitch of the same colour and to fill in the white background in whatever shade you prefer.

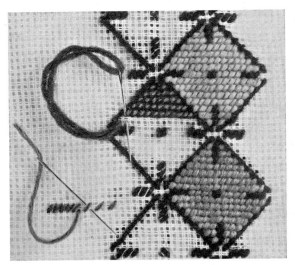

FIG. 75. Here is a close-up of the chair cover in Fig. 74, with two different methods of working tent-stitch

Even easier to work and richer in effect is the higher-priced canvas which has not only the design stencilled on, but one-way thread laid in position for you to couch over with tent stitch. This padding fills up well and makes double wool for working unnecessary. As a rule complete wools to finish the tapestry are included with these prepared stencils, so that the (at first sight) alarming price is not really so high after all.

Still another way in which fancy needlework shops sometimes smooth your path for you is by selling ready-worked designs in which you have only to fill in the background; but, of course, this is rather tame compared with doing the whole job yourself.

There is a great range of designs. They may be of the geo-metrical repeat kind, like the chair seat already described; they may have Victorian floral sprays; or they may be of the picture type, perhaps showing an old-world garden bright with flowers or a lady in crinoline and poke-bonnet. You have only to choose!

LOCKER RUG TAPESTRY

Perhaps this is hardly embroidery, for it is actually a modern way of rug-making by a method nearer to crochet than to fancy stitchery, but it gives a very tapestry-like result, as you will see by the stool cover in Fig. 76, is just as hard-wearing and a great deal quicker to do.

FIG. 76. Locker rug tapestry, in multi-coloured stripes, makes the cover for this stool

So if you love *petit point* but have not the leisure for it, try locker rug tapestry instead. It is thick and warm for chair and stool covers and small rugs, and in colouring can be just as gay as you please. It does not lend itself to picture designs, but you will soon invent for yourself plenty of geometrical patterns and striped effects.

It is worked, not with a sewing needle, but with a locker rug needle which costs a few pence from Messrs. Cox and Co., New Oxford Street, London, W.C.2, or from Dryad Handicrafts, St. Nicholas Street, Leicester. This tool is a large steel crochet hook with a needle eye at the unhooked end.

The method of working is very easy and ingenious. Use ordinary six-ply rug wool. For small items like the stool shown very little wool is needed.

You can use oddments left over from rugs, or twopenny hanks from the sixpenny stores, if you make a design in variegated stripes like the stool cover illustrated. It has five broad stripes, respectively of green, blue, yellow, pink and green, each stripe being divided from the next by a single line each of nigger-brown and white.

You will follow the plan easily from Fig. 76. Work across the short way on the usual rug canvas—preferably buff, not white.

To work with the locker needle, wind each colour of wool used into two separate balls of uneven size. Turn in two inches at one end of the canvas and work the first few rows through the double thickness to give a firm, neat edge.

Thread the end of the wool from the larger ball into the locker needle eye. *Leave the wool still attached to the ball.* Bring the needle up from underneath through a canvas hole at the end of a row. Pull through after it a workable length of wool. Keeping the ball underneath the canvas, dip the hook down into each hole in turn, catching up a loop of wool from the ball underneath. Continue till eight or ten loops are on the needle.

To lock these loops into place and pad them well, now draw the needle right through the loops, so that the wool in its eye passes under the loops, holding them firmly. Begin again, catching up loops, and continue similarly to the end of the row. Return by working the next row and so on.

When the locking thread in the needle is exhausted, take another from the second smaller ball of wool, neatly knotting or sewing the two ends together.

After a little practice you will be able to evolve many simple designs for yourself. As all rows are worked across, patterns in which the lines go this way also, rather than lengthwise, are easiest to carry out. Arrangements of checks are effective and not at all difficult.

CROSS-STITCH AND TAPESTRY STITCHES

Cross-stitch, which may be seen being worked in Fig. 70, is merely two slanting stroke-stitches laid over each other at right-angles to form a multiplication cross (×). It is so simple that you need no instructions for working it, except to remember to cross all stitches over the same way. This is ensured and working is quicker, when there is a row of cross-stitches to be done, if you work first all the single strokes on the same slant and then return by crossing them.

Tent-stitch, like a criminal, has many aliases! You may come across it under such names as half cross-stitch, *petit point*, needle-point and tapestry stitch. The first of these aliases exactly describes it, for it is actually the first half of a cross-stitch—a slanting stroke stitch, which, when worked on canvas, goes from one square into its (diagonal) neighbour.

Tent-stitch is *the* tapestry stitch, and nine out of ten pieces in this type of embroidery are executed in it. There are two ways of working it, both shown in Fig. 75.

The first and most usual method is seen being worked in dark double wool inside one of the diamonds. Make each half cross-stitch by bringing up the thread in a lower square of the two the stitch will cover, and then put it in the next upper square, bringing it out again in the square immediately beneath. In other words, work always with a straight, vertical set of the needle. Stitches will be upright on the wrong side.

This is the quickest method and the best for small areas of tapestry divided by other stitches running different ways (as the dark diamond outlines in Fig. 75) or for a few odd tent-stitches scattered in the work. But where large unbroken areas must be tent-stitched, as in so many tapestry pieces, you will find that this method of working, with the pull of the thread always on the diagonal, tends after a good many rows have been done to drag the embroidery sideways and spoil its shape.

Once this has happened, pressing and pulling are not of much avail to get it straight again, but this blemish will never occur if you work your tent-stitch in the second way, which is shown in light single wool, outside the diamonds, in Fig. 75.

Start as in the first method, by bringing the needle through in a lower square, but when inserting it in the next upper square do so diagonally, so that it comes out in the *next lower square but one* to that in which you started. Make this slanting insertion every time, thus working only every other stitch. Then return, also diagonally, filling in the stitches missed. This working plan gives slanting stitches on the wrong side also.

Couched Tent-stitch is the half cross-stitch worked over a separate matching laid thread, which it couches down. It is used when the wool is not thick enough to cover the canvas well and you do not want to use double wool. The locker-stitch described on page 138 is a form of this stitch done with a different implement.

Rice or Double Cross-stitch is an effective two-colour stitch used in both tapestry and cross-stitch embroidery. First work large cross-stitches covering four squares each way. Then, preferably with a finer thread and in a second colour, make a small cross-stitch over the intersection of each large one. The large crosses in Fig. 70 are in rice-stitch.

Tapestry Chain-stitch (sometimes aptly called Knitting-stitch) is an old tapestry stitch which is soft in effect and blends well. Consequently it is ideal to use for tapestry pieces which have a rather blurred flower design. Unlike other tapestry stitches, each row must start at the same end, as with ordinary chain-stitch, and there is no to-and-fro working.

Work as for chain-stitch (page 107), but take up one thread of the canvas at each stitch.

Chapter XIV

PRETTY DRESS EMBROIDERIES

NOWADAYS it is almost impossible to save money by making underwear at home, for the shops turn it out so very cheaply. But what one can do, for the price of a bought garment, is to make one which is of better material, more daintily sewn and with those telling touches of hand embroidery which would cost guineas, instead of shillings, if the garment was bought ready-made.

Again, a little hand stitchery is often the making of a blouse or frock, adding much both to its beauty and to its apparent cost. For children's clothes especially, there is simply no adornment like embroidery, for it wears and washes beautifully and yet costs far less than lace or bought trimmings.

Dress embroideries are enchanting to make. As only small quantities are used, they take very little time and yield the prettiest results.

Special dress uses for several of the types of embroidery already described in this book—appliqué, quilting, darning, cut-work, initials, wool embroidery and hem-stitching, for instance—have been mentioned and illustrated under their own headings in preceding pages. But there are certain types of embroidery which are used mainly or entirely as dress trimmings, and these deserve to have a chapter to themselves.

In general, when fashioning dress embroideries remember that they require the utmost daintiness of handling and stitchery. A little embroidery well done looks far better than more indifferently executed; in fact, even when it is well carried out, it is very easy to overdo embroidery on garments. Where more than a very little is used, mass it in one or two places, and you will get a far more artistic result. Thin, straggling effects are never very successful.

Practise any stitch you are not perfectly sure of, or cannot do smoothly, on an odd piece of the same material, with the same thread, before working it on the garment. Particularly with pale, dainty lingerie and babies' clothes, take special pains to keep both the material and your hands spotless, and to wrap the work in clean tissue paper the moment it is put aside.

Finish off very neatly too. This is partly for general pride of work, partly because the wrong side of a garment often shows when it is hung up, but mainly because good finishing stands the strain of laundering and ironing so much better.

FAGGOTING

I have insisted in Chapter XII on the many dress uses of hem-stitching when the material used is one from which threads can be drawn. Faggoting (sometimes called veining) is mock hem-stitching, serving much the same uses on non-draw-thread fabrics or where the decoration cannot follow the straight weave of the stuff.

It is used as a dainty join for minor seams, to attach separate or contrasting hems prettily or to form panels or lines of open-work trimming. You will want it occasionally for joining purposes when embroidering household items, but it is almost entirely a dress decoration.

There are several variations of faggoting, but for all of them the preliminary method of preparing the material is the same.

The regulation plan is to turn in and tack very narrow double hems along each of the edges to be joined, and this plan is very necessary on garments, such as underwear, which will be much laundered or, for the same reason, on washable household items like tray-cloths and runners.

On dresses, however, double hems are apt to make too much bulk. So, if such garments are not to be laundered, the usual plan is to make single turns only. If the material is one which frays badly, it may be necessary to overcast or pink these turns, but as a rule this precaution is not needed. Make the turns fairly wide, though—not much under $\frac{1}{2}$ in.

As the edges have to be tacked down to paper, it is a time-saver,

on suitable fabrics, to press the turn in with an iron, instead of
tacking it, and then to use your tacking to hold the two edges down

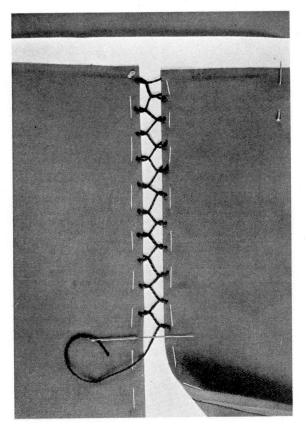

FIG. 77. Showing edges to be faggoted tacked down on paper and
buttonhole faggoting in progress

to the paper. As Fig. 77 shows you, the two edges must be placed
exactly the same distance apart—usually $\frac{1}{4}$ in.—all the way along.
This is to hold them firmly while the faggoting is being worked and
to ensure that it is of uniform width everywhere.

Use firm paper, either brown or white. I like squared arithmetic paper myself, as it makes it so easy to keep the two edges evenly apart. If you use unlined paper, do not try to tack by eye, but rule in two parallel lines to guide you. After a little practice,

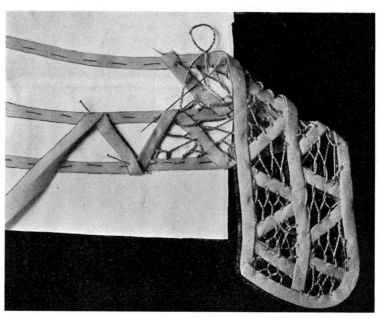

FIG. 78. The making of a collar from bias binding strips joined by diagonal faggoting. Both sides are shown

quite *short* seams may be held apart in an embroidery frame, but this is not a good plan for beginners or if the seam is of any length.

Sometimes, in order to enlarge a garment or other item or perhaps introduce a contrasting border, a hem is cut out quite separately and then faggoted on.

In this case, prepare the main edge as already described. For the hem, cut a straight strip or strips rather more than twice the finished width wanted, fold in half lengthwise, and then fold in the two raw edges to face and conceal each other. Tack this edge of the hem down on paper nearest to the other edge to be joined, and the faggoting stitches will then hold the two layers of the double hem together at the same time as they make the join.

Sometimes there is a fashion for a whole collar or yoke to be made by joining strips or flat tubes (called rouleaux) together by means of faggoting stitches. To do this, cut out the whole shape of the collar or yoke (not merely the half given in a paper pattern) and draw out on the paper whatever design of scrolls, curves or diagonals your strips or rouleaux are to follow.

Either make rouleaux of self-material or use ready-made silk bias binding, folding this just as explained above for a separate hem; the advantage here is that the creases are already made for you. Lay the folded strips or rouleaux along the lines of your pattern, as in Fig. 78, and tack down. Having thus provided the framework, hold it all together with faggoting. The illustration shows how the stitches must be varied in size and direction to fit the differing shapes in various parts of the pattern.

When all stitchery is done, whether on a seam, added hem or collar, untack the work from the paper and press it.

For faggoting stitches see page 150.

SMOCKING

Smocked bags are occasionally seen, and I once smocked a short white curtain with excellent effect, but this embroidery is really entirely for dress purposes. Though it only consists of very simple embroidery stitches worked over gathers instead of flat material, it is extraordinarily graceful in effect.

It is popular for children's clothes, and at times has a great vogue for adult dresses, blouses and overalls in pliable, thin materials such as soft silks and cottons. Seersucker (Fig. 79), voile (Fig. 80) and crêpe de Chine smock particularly well.

Owing to the fullness needed, smocking would be too bulky if worked on thick fabrics (except, perhaps, in very narrow panels); but, also owing to the fullness, smocked garments are very elastic.

They almost seem to grow with a child, and have just the colourful simplicity to suit very little folk. In fact, this is essentially a youthful decoration, even when worn by grown-up people.

Its success largely depends on the care and exactness with which the material is prepared for smocking.

Putting in the Gathers. A garment must be gathered first of all,

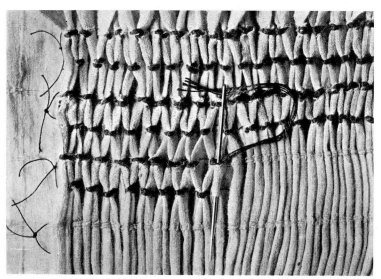

FIG. 79. Honeycombing being worked on seersucker. Note gathering threads tied in pairs

directly after cutting out, and before joining the front to the yoke or shoulder. As many rows of gathers have to be put in very evenly, it is easiest to use as a guide a smocking transfer, which consists of rows of dots very exactly placed. The distance between the rows and the dots themselves varies on different transfers. Remember when choosing one that the larger these distances are the more material the smocking will need and the fuller and more elastic the finished garment will be.

To preserve slim lines, modern smocking is usually done on

quite shallow gathers. If the transfer used provides for wider ones, you can diminish them by picking up between each two dots as well as at each dot itself. A comparatively bulky stuff, such as a thin woollen like nuns' veiling, should be set in shallower gathers than a thin fabric.

Cut off as much of the transfer as is needed, allowing one or two more rows than the depth required, as the embroidery will set better if the top and bottom rows are not used. Iron off the needed portion of the transfer on to the *wrong* side of the stuff.

With contrasting cotton, gather in parallel rows along the dots, using a separate thread for each row. Leave a long, loose thread at the end of each row. When all gathering is done, pull up the threads to the finished width wanted, and secure them by knotting every two threads together, as in Fig. 79 (extreme left). Be careful to give all rows exactly the same tension, except round a neckline, when each row is a little looser than the last to give the curve.

Another way of securing the threads, preferred by many people, is to put in a pin upright between two rows, at the end, and wind the threads of those two rows together round the pin several times.

The end-on pleats formed by the gathers will lie more evenly— or rather, stand up more evenly—if you stroke the gathers. To do this, you must temporarily draw up the threads quite tightly with pins. Holding the gathers with the left thumb and forefinger, stroke downwards with the side of the needle in each fold in turn. Afterwards let out the gathers to the required width.

The material is now ready for smocking. It is generally prettiest to use several different stitches in one piece of work, as in Fig. 80, and much of the charm of this stitchery lies in the many different arrangements that can be made even with only three or four stitches. Honeycombing, however, is best worked alone, as in Fig. 79, as it requires a number of successive rows to show it at its best.

Smocking stitches (see page 151) are so simple that you can hardly go wrong with them, but it takes some practice to do them with the precision which gives them most beauty.

After working, finish off the smocking as described in Chapter XIX.

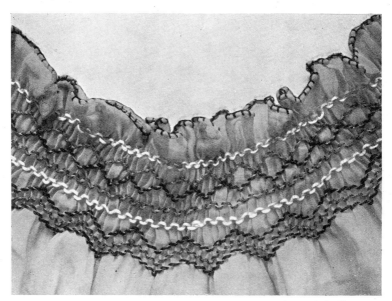

FIG. 80. Circular smocking on voile, in single cable (white lines) and wave-stitch

EMBROIDERED WAYS FOR UNDERWEAR

Appliqué on net (Fig. 81) is not included with the other varieties of appliqué in Chapter V because it is exclusively a dress embroidery. It makes a beautiful and fragile-looking decoration for underwear and night wear, but in reality, when properly worked, it has much durability and will wear and wash for a long time.

It is suitable for thin and delicate materials which would not take such embroideries as *broderie anglaise* or cut-work.

The name, appliqué on net, is not really very accurate. What actually happens is that a double net hem is prepared, as described on page 144 for an added hem that is to be faggoted on. The net hem, however, has the raw edge of the garment—say, the top edge of a slip—sandwiched between its two layers and held there by hand or machine stitching.

Choose a flowing appliqué border design, and iron this off on to

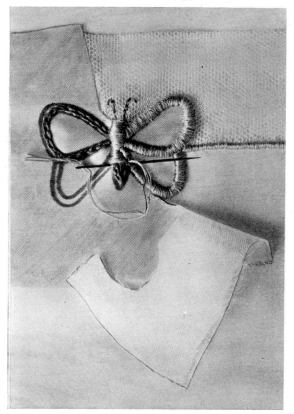

FIG. 81. Here a net hem is joined to an undie with cord-stitch and a satin butterfly is appliquéd on and the surplus edges cut away

an oddment of satin or the underwear material. Cut out the design with tiny turnings. Tack it into place over the join of net and

11—(C.104)

garment, so that half the design will appear on each fabric and the join will be wholly or mostly covered. Fold in the turnings as you tack. Then pad and buttonhole-stitch the outlines as for cut-work (Chapter IX).

An alternative plan is to leave big turnings round the design, and cut these away close up to the buttonholing when the embroidery is done, after the manner of embroidered appliqués (Fig. 81).

If you want merely to work a centre-front motif or spray which will cover only a small part of the join of net hem and garment, the join itself should be made decoratively. Tack the net hem over the garment edge, and then work all along the join in cord-stitch (page 74) or couching (page 43). See Fig. 81.

Lace yokes, edgings or insets may be daintily joined on to underwear in a similar way. Tack the edge of the lace over the garment, overlapping it by a good ½ in. Embroider over the join with cord-stitch, afterwards closely cutting away the raw edges of the garment or the material under the lace in the case of an inset. If the lace itself has a slightly raised edge, as often with needle-run designs, the cord-stitch need not be padded before working the satin-stitch.

Faggoting and Smocking Stitches

As faggoting is mock hem-stitching, most faggoting stitches simulate more or less closely one or other of the better-known hem-stitches.

Bar Faggoting imitates double or bar hem-stitch. Having prepared the material edges and tacked them to paper as described earlier in this chapter, bring the needle up from the wrong side in one edge and take a straight bar- or stroke-stitch across the space into the edge opposite, inserting the needle there from the right side to the wrong. Pull the needle through and return by twisting the thread twice round the bar-stitch from left to right.

Insert the needle in the first edge where it started, and slip it through the fold invisibly for ¼ in.; then bring it through and start the second bar.

Diagonal Faggoting (Fig. 78) imitates diagonal hem-stitch. Bring up the needle in one hem or fold, and take a stitch across into the opposite edge, from the *underside upwards*, not opposite the first stitch but diagonally across the opening. Put the needle *under* the stitch just made, then take another stitch diagonally across to the first edge. Repeat all along, working diagonally into each edge alternately.

Buttonhole Faggoting (Fig. 77) also gives a result very like diagonal hem-stitch, but is rather softer and less tailored-looking than diagonal faggoting, which makes it specially pretty on children's clothes. It is also very easy. Simply work a spaced buttonhole-stitch down the "run" (space), taking a stitch into each edge alternately as shown in the illustration.

Smocking stitches are numerous. Here are some of the prettiest and best-wearing.

Honeycombing (Fig. 79) is unlike all other smocking stitches, which lie entirely on the surface, in that most of this stitch is hidden in the pleats. It is quickly worked and very elastic—the last a point to be considered when decorating children's clothes.

Work on two rows of gathers at once, beginning at the top left-hand corner and working from left to right as shown. With a back-stitch catch together the first two pleats in the upper row. Return the needle to the wrong side, not catching any other pleat when doing this, and slip it down the pleat it is in (Fig. 79), bringing it out in that same pleat on the level of the gathered thread beneath.

Back-stitch this pleat and the next together, slip invisibly up the second of these two pleats (the third from the start) to the upper row, and so continue up and down, alternately slipping and back-stitching. Remember that the second pleat in one back-stitch always becomes the first pleat in the next back-stitch either up or down.

Of smocking stitches proper, outline, single cable and herring-bone form narrow lines excellent for the top row of a panel or to divide more important stitches, while wave and Vandyke stitches, like honeycombing, make wider and more decorative patterns.

Outline-stitch is worked as described on page 26. Bring the needle through from the wrong side in a pleat and take one stitch over each pleat. This stitch has little "give," so that it is useful at the top or where a firm holding line is needed.

Single Cable-stitch (two rows of it in white are shown in Fig. 80). Working from left to right, go along a gathered row, taking a back-stitch in each row, with the thread *under* the needle for the first stitch, *above* it for the second stitch and so on alternately. The result is a fascinating linked chain effect, very quickly worked.

Herringbone-stitch should be worked as described on page 153, with one stitch to each pleat, and the centre of each stitch over the gathering thread. This stitch is a little heavy in effect, so use only single rows sparingly. It has great elasticity and for this reason combines in a practical way with honeycombing.

Double Cable-stitch is the narrowest and least conspicuous of the more imposing stitches. It is merely two rows of single cable stitch worked close together, almost touching. When working the second row, reverse the above and below of the thread compared with the first row. The result is a thicker chain effect than in single cable, with the alternate middle links twice as thick as the outer ones.

Wave-stitch is well shown in Fig. 80, in each case just below the white single cable stitch. It forms diamonds near the top and zigzag waves at the bottom of the smocking.

Work from left to right. Bring the needle up from the wrong side between the first and second pleats. With the thread below the needle take up the first pleat, and then the second, drawing the two slightly together (not closely). To form the waves, next draw together the second and third pleats at a slightly higher level; then the third and fourth a little higher again, till the fourth and fifth are level with the next gathering thread above the start and form the top point of a wave. Descend similarly to the starting level, now keeping the thread *above* the needle.

To make diamonds instead of waves, the second row should reverse the ascending and descending of the first row.

Vandyke Stitch gives a lot of effect for not much work. It is really visible honeycombing. Work as for honeycombing, but take the thread upwards or downwards on the *right* side between each two back-stitches, so that it shows and forms part of the pattern, instead of hiding it in the pleat in the honeycomb way.

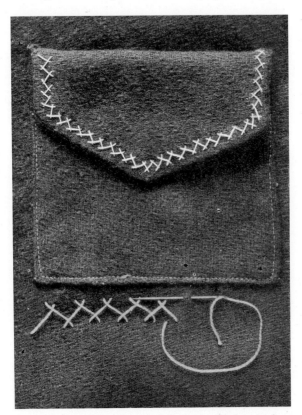

FIG. 82. *Above*, child's pocket flap trimmed with herringbone-stitch
Below, the stitch being worked

OTHER PRETTY STITCHES FOR DRESS EMBROIDERIES

Herringbone-stitch (Fig. 82) is used in both plain sewing and embroidery. The illustration shows it forming a simple decoration for a child's pocket; it may go round collars and cuffs in the same way. It is the only stitch used for the very dainty shadow embroidery described in Chapter XV. Also, if worked in a wide line in rather substantial thread, it makes a very dainty open casing through which to run underwear ribbons or those on babies' little garments. It is sometimes used as a minor smocking stitch (page 151).

This stitch is worked from left to right, along two imaginary parallel lines, or across the outline (in shadow embroidery). The working is shown at the bottom of Fig. 82. Starting at the left end of the uppermost line, take the thread forward and downward on a diagonal slant to the lower line, and take a small horizontal stitch *backward* along that line. Then return by slanting forward to the upper line, making another backward stitch here. Continue by taking a small backward stitch on each line alternately.

Feather-stitch (Fig. 83) in its several varieties is particularly a dress decoration, though it has a few uses also in other kinds of embroidery. These are noted below under each type of feather-stitch. When you want a simple trimming for babies' or children's clothes, to edge the little collars, cuffs, yokes or hems or as an adornment between groups of narrow tucks, one of the feather-stitches has the right charming simplicity.

Feather-stitches also work in well with various outline-stitches to form the sort of ornamental borders described in Chapter III.

The feather-stitches belong to the buttonhole-stitch group and, like them, must all be worked with the thread *held down under the needle*. Three of the best varieties are illustrated in Fig. 83.

Simple or Vein Feather-stitch (centre, Fig. 82) has the dress uses mentioned above. It is also an effective way of working the veins of leaves—hence its second name—or, in outline embroidery, groups of fine, feathery foliage. In dressmaking, it is used for flannel fells on babies' woollen garments.

Bring the needle through from the wrong side at the top of the line or hem to be worked. Take a slanting stitch by putting the needle in from the right side nearly $\frac{1}{4}$ in. to the right of where it first came up, and bringing it out again on the working line farther down, as in the illustration. Draw up, keeping the thread *under* the needle. Make a similar slanting stitch on the left, its top level with the bottom of the last stitch, and so on alternately.

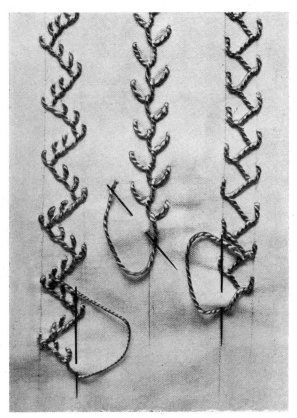

FIG. 83. Feather-stitches
Left, treble; *Centre*, simple or vein; *Right*, triangular

Double and Treble Feather-stitches (the treble is shown in Fig. 83, left-hand stitch). These are variations of triangular feather-stitch (Fig. 83, right-hand stitch) for use when wider and more showy lines of embroidery are wanted.

Work just as explained for the triangular feather-stitch described below, with these differences—

(*a*) Treble feather-stitch, as illustrated. Take three stitches on each side before crossing over to the other, and place these stitches so that their connecting purl or corded edge forms slants, making the finished effect a series of right-angles.

(*b*) Double feather-stitch is worked as for the treble type, but with only two stitches on each side instead of three.

Triangular Feather-stitch (Fig. 83, right-hand stitch) is perhaps the most important variety. It has rather a tailored, straight-line effect, so that it is useful for finishing the hems of items with rather formal embroidery designs or for edging round crazy patchwork. It is this variety which is sometimes used as a minor smocking stitch or for working as a finish down each edge of a smocked panel.

Fig. 83 (right-hand stitch) shows the working of the stitch, which is done downwards as for the simple feather-stitch, but with each stitch taken vertically instead of slanting inwards towards the centre. Start each stitch level with the bottom of the preceding one and work very evenly to get the proper formal effect.

Coral-stitch gives a pretty knotted outline that looks well on children's or other clothes. Another and picturesque name for it is Snail Trail. It goes well round even elaborate curves or spirals, and is an effective outline stitch where a rather broken-up look is wanted. In fact, you will find it useful in many ways!

At the right-hand end of the line bring the thread up from the wrong side. Hold the thread down for a little distance along the line and, while so doing, pick up a small stitch, which passes under the line and the held-down thread, making the stitch in a forward and slanting direction. Pull up, thus forming a straight stitch ending in a knot. Repeat all along.

CHAPTER XV

MINOR FORMS OF EMBROIDERY

EMBROIDERY is influenced by fashion only a degree less than dress and furnishing styles. Certain types of stitchery, often for no explainable reason, will not "catch on" at certain times. I remember a few years ago discovering in the United States, and proudly bringing home with me, lovely specimens of quilting. In America this was so popular that even the five- and ten-cent stores were selling the ready-stamped designs, but to my disappointment no one in England would look at them!

Since then, as you know, quilting has had the same vogue over here as in America. I was before the fashion, that's all.

And so, in titling this chapter, I use the phrase "Minor Forms of Embroidery" as a short way of saying, "Forms of embroidery which are of minor importance at the time of writing." They are not having a great vogue at the present time, because they are not the fashion of the moment, are not the type of embroidery ever likely to be very widely popular (like certain "highbrow" books and music), or are new and very little known.

But at any time to come—perhaps even by the date this book is published—any of these now comparatively unimportant types of embroidery may leap into sudden popularity, so that you want to know urgently how to make them. In that case this chapter may easily become, for you, the most important in this book.

Or you may be one of those home embroideresses who have originality and the spirit of adventure. You do not want to make just what a thousand other women are making, but like something rather less hackneyed. In that case I hope that this chapter will open new doorways—and pleasant ones—for you, showing you stitchery which has not yet (and perhaps never will) become the popular craze.

157

NEEDLE ETCHING

Never was there a more apt name than this, for, as Fig. 84 shows you, this modern type of embroidery gives, with the needle,

FIG. 84. This old inn forms a perfect subject for needle etching, in outline-stitch with a single strand of stranded cotton

a perfect illusion of a fine etching. Such a chance to be a first-rate artist without even being able to draw!

I have seen needle etching used to adorn such household items as luncheon-table mats, and, whatever it is used for, it is always more or less effective. But it imitates a picture so completely and faithfully that to my mind it should be used only as real etchings are used—to frame and hang them on the wall—or perhaps as the cover of a blotter or book. Isn't there something incongruous and Vandal-like in eating off an etching?

To maintain the illusion, which is almost undetectable when the embroidery is framed and hung, subjects with the detail and delicacy of an etching are chosen. Simple landscapes are good; old buildings, such as cathedrals or historic houses, with their wealth of fine architecture, are better. It is not easy to find suitable transfers, but every art needlework shop sells, at low prices, envelopes each containing an attractive design ready stamped on beige linen and a skein of dark brown stranded cotton for working it.

To keep the etching idea, always use this sort of colouring, such as one gets in an actual picture. The whole piece of work is embroidered in one colour and also in one stitch—outline-stitch—though occasionally it is convenient to use stroke-stitch for tiny details. Long-sighted people may find the work tryingly close, but for those who are patient and enjoy detail this embroidery is fascinating to do and gives extremely artistic results.

Any picture-framer will stretch the finished work properly for you over cardboard or plywood, and frame it correctly in a narrow moulding or passe-partout.

MAP EMBROIDERY (FIG. 85)

Somewhat akin to needle etching, in subject at least, is the embroidering of maps. If wanderlust is part of your make-up, you will get a definite thrill out of perpetuating, in needlework, enchanting parts of the world which you have either visited or hope to visit. Even if you are one of those who agree that "East, west, home's best," you will like the variety of stitchery and colouring that make up an embroidered map of the picture type (Fig. 85).

If the right transfer is not obtainable, it is an easy matter to do without it. Draw or trace your design from an actual large-scale map (tracing requires no artistic ability at all), and then transfer it to your material by the method given in Chapter III, page 20. It gives a more graphic, amusing effect if you can draw enough to substitute appropriate little sketches for some or all of the place names, as in the map of California illustrated. But if not,

FIG. 85. An effective map worked in many-coloured crewel wools in a
mixture of outline and solid stitches

a very attractive map may be made by neatly lettering in the place names (see Chapter XI for hints on doing this) and merely working such easily drawn geographical features as—

Mountains—outline humps or triangles.

Forests—groups of trees each consisting of a green triangle, point upwards, mounted on a brown stem.

Coast line—a narrow belt of green or gold satin-stitch, with one or two blue outlines outside it to represent water depths.

Sunset in the west—a solid red half-circle with fiery rays jutting out from it and two wavy lines below representing waves.

And so on.

Be sure to have an imposing title in an unoccupied upper corner. Good bold lettering for this, please! Chapter XI will give you suggestions for both the lettering and a surround to enclose it. If it is a cruise or voyage your needle is commemorating, put the ship in somewhere—traced, say, from a picture post card.

Maps can be treated more individually than most kinds of embroidery, but in general a neutral-coloured, dull-surfaced background, very simple stitchery, and plenty of varied colour give a pleasing effect. You will notice in Fig. 85 how well solid bits of embroidery are contrasted with light outline working. The map is worked in fine wools of fourteen different colours—most of them bright—on beige linen, but cotton (not silk) threads would be equally good.

For island maps I like the island to be a linen appliqué on a background of deep blue linen or shantung silk; be sure to choose a blue which does not go dark and dull by artificial light. The contrast of the appliqué gives colour and life to a simple map that is merely lettered and not pictured, by the way.

Whatever material is used, cut it considerably larger than the map size, to allow for a worked border, and outside that at least two inches all round for mounting. The simple border in Fig. 85 is merely four spaced rows of outline-stitch in varying colourings, with a row of lighter simple feather-stitch worked between the two middle lines.

The map should be mounted and framed in the same way as a needle etching (page 159).

SHADOW EMBROIDERY (FIG. 86)

Do not confuse this most dainty and delicate of embroideries

FIG. 86. Shadow embroidery: *Left*, wrong side; *Right*, right side

with shadow quilting, described in Chapter VI. The two have nothing in common but their enchantingly pretty veiled effect.

Shadow or Etruscan embroidery consists in working a design on the *wrong* side of transparent material—organdie, generally—so that the stitches and colours show through to the right side in a subdued, shadowy way. It is charming and hard-wearing for adorning items which can be carried out in organdie, such as luncheon-table and dressing-table mats (for modern light, not dark, furniture), night-gown and pyjama sachets, small cushion covers, and babies' fairy-like little bonnets and frocks.

As embroidering is done *across* the various parts of the design, choose a transfer which is broken up into long, narrow spaces. For instance, most floral designs with daisies or long slender leaves are suitable. Stamp the transfer rather lightly on to the *wrong* side of the organdie, remembering that a somewhat cool iron is best for this material, which quickly curls under heat.

Use a flat embroidery thread which spreads out well; three strands of stranded cotton are excellent. Get colours strongly contrasting with the material, and definitely brighter than you want them, as the organdie through which they are seen will soften them a good deal. Usually, shadow embroidery looks best worked all in one colour, which should be bright or full in tone, on a white or pale organdie.

Only one stitch is used—the herringbone (see page 153). Work this *across* all the petals, leaves and so on, and work it rather closely. The result, on the right side, is that the design is outlined in neat back-stitch (the stitches not quite touching) with blurred colour showing through between the outlines in the prettiest way. If the design has any fine stems or lines not given in double outline, work these from the right side in slightly spaced back-stitch to match the right-side effect of the herringboning.

Owing to the transparency of the material, care must be taken to start and finish off each thread very neatly. Start with the smallest possible knot. A good way of finishing off is to work over a back-stitch twice.

In Fig. 86 the material is folded over to show (left) the wrong side with the stitchery, and (right) the shadow effect and back-stitched outlines on the right side.

SHADED FLOWER EMBROIDERY (FIG. 87)

Nowadays this really beautiful work is not much seen, for it needs plenty of time and patience and not a little artistic skill. If you have the leisure and courage to attempt it, however, it will bring you rich dividends from its lovely results and the satisfaction of having created real beauty.

It will also teach you more, perhaps, than any other type of stitchery described in this book, about the skilful blending of tones and colours and the fashioning of exquisite stitches.

One might call this work "needle colour-photography," for it

FIG. 87. Shaded flower embroidery (with appliqué bowl) on dark grey sateen

imitates with exquisite exactness Nature's own painting and shading of tints. The designs used are mostly of flowers—hence the name—but birds and butterflies may also appear in them. This is solid embroidery, almost entirely in satin-stitch or its variations, and as every colour and every shade of that colour must be accurately placed to simulate Nature, a very large range of tones is needed.

This embroidery is not very cheap, anyway, owing to the number of threads used, and it is usually worth the slight extra expense of working with real silk, though such threads as silky stranded cotton also gives good results. Threads should be soft and flat, so that they will cover the surface well.

Remember that whereas in outline and other simple embroideries definite contrast is aimed at in choosing, say, two blues for flowers, here you are imitating natural gradations of colour, which are often almost imperceptible. So it may be necessary to have a skein each of every blue in that particular range of tones. I emphasize this because so many easy modern embroideries depend so much on strong contrast for their effect that after working them a great deal you may need to train your eye to the delicate variations between one shade and its nearest darker or lighter neighbour.

For instance, four different shades are blended even for the comparatively small flower petals in Fig. 87. It is a good plan to practise first of all by making a drawing or getting a spray of a flower that is in season, and to keep it in front of you for copying the colouring while you do the work—also to take it with you to the shop when buying your silks. This sort of careful observation soon trains your eye and gives you beautiful results.

Work small or unshaded portions of the design in satin-stitch (page 73) and all large shaded parts in its variation known as long-and-short or Kensington stitch. The latter is described on page 169. For very large parts, which would be very laborious if carried out entirely in stitchery, an appliqué may be used, as for the bowl in Fig. 87.

Work shaded flower embroidery on material with a soft, somewhat shiny texture. Linen is unsuitable, but a sturdy silk or sateen, backed with a thin cotton to enable it to carry the rather heavy stitchery, gives the right results. The soft, glowing look of the work, with its multitude of shades, is thrown up best, incidentally, by a dark background. Black satin is nearly always effective, and so is the dark grey sateen against which the pale yellow bowl and rosy-pink flowers in the illustration show up so bravely.

The best teacher for this kind of fancy-work is experience, which shows you many a subtle point, many a clever trick with needle or thread, as you go along. It is worth remembering, however, from the start that the deep tones in flowers are usually near their centres, most petals paling towards the outer edges. Half-closed buds, again, are deeper in shade than fully opened blossoms.

Nor is it always merely a question of choosing a deeper or paler tone in the same range. You can give the effect of sunlight on a particular blossom by working it in a shade of its own colour which contains a tone of yellow; whereas flowers or leaves in shadow take on a bluer note. A dark background makes the threads look more vivid; a pale or white one robs them of a little of their colour.

As shaded flower embroidery is slow to do and does not wash very satisfactorily, keep it for very special items which will not soil quickly or have heavy wear. If they can be under glass, as for needlework pictures, or showing through glass-topped dressing-tables or trays, so much the better. It is beautiful work for silk evening shawls, very special cushion covers or for church embroidery.

Start with something small. When you have gained experience and become fascinated with the exquisite results, you can go on to a more ambitious piece of work.

Ribbon and Tape Embroideries

These are miscellaneous in character and all very simple and quick, for tape or ribbon, used as a thread, soon covers a design or forms a broadly effective pattern. Tape embroideries usually wash like the proverbial rags.

Ribbon Work had a great vogue about thirty years ago—deservedly so, for it was both speedy and pretty. The idea was to use a special thin baby ribbon as a thread, making each petal of, say, a daisy design with a single ribbon stroke-stitch. Smaller details were worked in ordinary embroidery stitches.

The special ribbon used is now very difficult to obtain. Ordinary ribbons, with their ridged edges, are not suitable, but you can get very pretty results by using either the soft shaded ribbon sometimes sold very cheaply for lingerie or silk braid of suitable width. The background material must be loosely woven enough for this extra large "thread" to pass through—a condition fulfilled by many woollens of a tweedy persuasion.

Ribbon or Tape Appliqués. When a design consists partly or

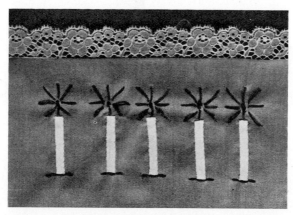

FIG. 88. On this night-gown the twinkling candles are quickly made tape appliqués

wholly of narrow, straight strips, such as the candles in Fig. 88, it is very effective if covered with narrow tape or ribbon appliqués. These have the advantage of two ready-finished edges, which need no turning in, and are quickly applied either by blind appliqué (page 38) or by couching (page 43).

You will also find it easy to make simple little designs, of the kind needed for trimming underwear or children's clothes, which lend themselves to tape appliqués. For instance, make stick-like little figures such as small children draw for themselves—a line for the body, a bent one for each arm and leg, etc.—and make up a group marching in line, fighting or shaking hands. Toddlers love such elementary, lively "pictures" on their rompers or feeders.

They are very simple to work—narrow tape appliqués for the limbs (folded over at elbow and knee to the correct bend), a wider one for each body and a round head with features in outline-stitch, with French knot eyes. Or cut an appliqué long enough for head and body in one and gather it near the top to represent the neck before hemming it down.

Tape is effective in either black or white on bright colours. If

Fig. 89. On loosely woven woollens, simple embroidery with the narrowest French tape is attractive

the appliqués themselves are to be coloured, you must home-dye white tape or use sturdy washing ribbon.

Tape Darning (Fig. 89). This is a handsome, rather tailored-looking trimming for dresses and summer coats in loose-weave woollens and linens. Use the simplest of border patterns or motifs, such as you can make up as you go along—Fig. 89 shows a sample of each—darning them in in the narrowest French tape. The French variety is chosen from no unpatriotic motives, but because it is narrower ($\frac{1}{8}$ in.) than the English makes.

Any tape cross-stitches used (see the motif in the illustration) should have their intersections held down with small contrasting crosses made in embroidery silk.

A variation for household items like runners, tray-cloths and cushions is to withdraw runs of threads from linen, either in rows or in 2-in. squares or slightly larger oblongs. Make the runs wide enough to take very narrow tape and weave this in and out of them with a bodkin, making the tape stitches on the right side longer than the spaces of run between them.

STITCHES FOR SHADED FLOWER EMBROIDERY

Long-and-Short Satin-stitch is *the* shading stitch, as it blends in various tones so smoothly and naturally (if well worked) that the eye cannot see where one begins and the other ends. It is also used, even in one-colour embroidery, where the surface to be covered is too large for a single line of satin-stitch.

Another use for it is not sufficiently known, considering its effectiveness and comparative quickness. When you are working designs which are too large to look well purely in outline and would take too long, or be too heavy, if solidly filled in, try making a broad outline with one row only of this stitch, leaving the centre parts vacant or with markings merely outlined. The effect is of an irregular buttonhole-stitch, but without the corded edge.

Long-and-short stitch is very simple, but you will find a little practice is needed to get smooth, well-blended results. Work a first row of satin-stitch with one end of each stitch coming to the outline, but on the inner edge the stitches all of irregular lengths, long, short or medium, without any plan. The next row (worked in a different tone in shaded embroidery) is irregular along both edges. Thus its first edge is worked to fit into and somewhat overlap the irregularities of the first row worked, while the second edge creates a similar jagged line into which the third row is worked.

Continue row after row until the outline is filled, changing shades as required. Thanks to the uneven working, the rows will "melt" into each other without showing any joining line.

Laid Filling is really all-over couching. It is a quick and handsome way of filling large outlines, but as the stitch is rather exposed and not very hard-wearing it should generally be used for embroidery which will be protected by glass.

Floss silk or all six strands of stranded cotton are the most suitable threads, as they spread well, with a finer silk or fewer strands of stranded cotton for the catching stitches.

First lay the wide threads. To do this, make a very long stroke stitch straight across. Bring the needle up to the right side again on the same outline, but $\frac{1}{8}$ in. away and take a return stroke-stitch across. This leaves a space between the two stitches. Continue back and forth in this way and then return, filling all the spaces similarly.

Using finer thread, now hold down all the laid stitches with tiny bar-stitches, as in ordinary couching. The bar-stitches may be made either at regular intervals, alternating in each row, or veins and markings may be worked in them, if these markings are well enough distributed to hold down the laid threads all over the surface. The latter plan is used for the leaves in Fig. 97, page 186.

Chapter XVI

OLD-WORLD EMBROIDERIES

EVERY woman who makes a hobby of fancy stitchery is not only an individual creator of needle beauty, but one of a long procession of embroideresses which stretches centuries back into the dim history of the craft. All of us, as we ply our busy needles, must wonder sometimes about those other needlewomen of long ago and the things which they, too, sat and stitched.

Sometimes, in museums, at exhibitions of antiques, in second-hand shops, we come across embroideries which were old before we, or our mothers or grandmothers, were born. If we are lucky, among our old family treasures we have other specimens, their colours mellowed by time, with empty spaces where threads have rotted out or moths have attacked. We may know something of their history, or ignorance of it may set us guessing as to those earlier marchers in the long embroidery procession. From their faded work we get glimpses of their lives and the times in which they sewed, study their materials and stitches and perhaps copy, in our modern colours, some of those old designs.

If you have imagination, the history of embroidery must appeal to you. You may like to start a modest collection of old examples. I am not suggesting that you should wade through endless tomes on the subject, but you will want to know how to recognize the specimens you come across, judge of their age and period and know whether they are worth acquiring. A few old embroideries have been revived in recent years, and when you are working them yourself their ancient story becomes doubly interesting.

In this one chapter I cannot hope to give you a great deal of information about embroidery antiques—only a few notes on those you are most likely to come across. If you want to know more with very little labour or expense, I can heartily recommend the various picture books on English embroideries of different periods

171

obtainable from the Victoria and Albert Museum in London or from H.M. Stationery Office in London, Edinburgh, Manchester, Cardiff and Belfast. They cost only 6d. each and are full of interesting photographs with an explanatory introduction.

SAMPLERS

Perhaps these "samples" of different stitches by which little girls of many generations learnt to embroider seem to us the most romantic of all old embroideries. Really old ones are seldom met with outside museums, but as samplers were in vogue for about two and a half centuries (roughly, from 1600 to 1850) the later specimens are often seen, frequently in very good condition.

I cannot make the last remark about the one shown in Fig. 90, which is distinctly decrepit. It was made in 1834 (most samplers not prohibitive in price nowadays are of about this date) by Mary Ann ——. Her last name is obliterated by moths, which took very kindly to the fine woollen canvas on which it was worked! By this same woollen canvas and by all the little designs and verse being worked in cross-stitch, you would know it for a late Georgian or early Victorian sampler even if it were not dated—though actually name and date are another feature of about a hundred years ago.

If, in a museum or elsewhere, you have the luck to see earlier samplers, made between about 1600 and 1750, you will notice various differences. They are probably on linen, somewhat long and narrow in shape (strips, rather than oblongs) and with formal patterns (not the trees and birds beloved by Mary Ann ——) arranged in bands across the linen. All sorts of stitches, including drawn-thread ones, were practised on these early samplers, and one wonders why the little girls of later generations were confined so strictly to cross-stitch!

Here is a tip if you want a sampler and have little money to spend. Buy one less than a century old and you will get it a great deal cheaper than one which is only a year or two over that age. The reason is that needlework a hundred years old or more can be taken into the United States duty free and is consequently in

Jesus permit thy Gracious name to stand

As the first efforts of an infants hand

And while her fingers o'er the canvass move

Engage her tender heart to seek thy love

Mary Ann
Aged 10 Years
1834

FIG. 90. A late Georgian sampler complete with verse, birds, a
wreath of leaves and a whole forest of trees

great demand among American visitors. This sends up the price, whereas if you buy a sampler dated ninety or ninety-five years ago, you have only to keep it a few years and it will then be of a most respectable antiquity!

Samplers look their best in gold or narrow, shiny black frames. If you can find an old-fashioned and rather shabby frame of this kind, probably holding some worthless Victorian picture, it will make a more appropriate setting for the old needlework than something modern.

Modern Samplers. To some extent samplers have come back into vogue during recent years, but they are no longer practice pieces for children—merely a fashion among older embroideresses. They are always cross-stitched, but mostly substitute a verse for the frequent Victorian alphabet; otherwise they follow old models closely.

An attractive new idea is to work a sampler in red and white on a black felt background. Another is to design yourself, or buy ready-prepared, one which commemorates a special private or public event. For instance, a private one might represent your garden, with little flowers, trees, birds in true sampler style, also such features as a sun-dial or tennis court, if you have it, and your favourite garden verse.

As an example of a "public event" sampler, one woman's magazine designed a delightful one to celebrate the Silver Jubilee of the King in 1935.

Old Tapestry and Beadwork

Both tapestry and beadwork (they have many points in common) were very popular during the whole Victorian era, and more or less dilapidated specimens of both are found in many homes and are still quite cheap to buy, though they are beginning to rank as antiques.

Tapestry is so very strong and durable that most Victorian examples are mainly in good condition, even if they have seen decades of service on an old-fashioned chair or foot-stool. They are mostly worked in stylized flower groups or formal geometrical designs which look well with very modern, straight-line furniture. So they should not be folded away as museum pieces, but turned to up-to-date use. Chair-seat covers are always wanted and even foot-stools are now, like other things Victorian, back in fashion. Or the work may be utilized for small cushion covers or for handbags.

FIG. 91. A comparatively harmless specimen of Victorian combined tapestry and
beadwork

An attractive fashion of the last century, not copied in modern work, was to tent-stitch most of the design in wool, but to throw up high-lights here and there by working them in silk, which gave a bright gleam to those small portions. The effect was charming, and those long-ago embroideresses could not know that the silk would perish long before the wool, and fall out, leaving naked white canvas patches. You will find this sign of age on many tapestries of sixty or seventy years ago.

Fortunately it is quite easy to repair them for use to-day, as the rotted silk parts were only a very small portion of the whole. Fill them in either with a thick real silk thread or with wool and they will probably last another sixty years! You will have to guess at the original colour, but may be sure that it was a pale one —probably white or cream, to give the effect of light. In any case, only pale or faded tints would look right in these old designs which are softened by time.

Beadwork, which came to England from Germany, like many

other German things, with the Prince Consort, Queen Victoria's husband, had a background worked in tapestry, while the design was carried out in dark, white and silvery glass beads, each laboriously back-stitched into place (Fig. 91). Often the designs were rather atrocious affairs, mingling shaded stylized flowers with geometrical borders, and the whole effect, except for some of the small handbags, was heavy and ugly. It was used chiefly for footstools and fire-screens.

But now time has toned down the crude colours and given beadwork specimens a certain antique charm. If of no use in their original form, they may be framed for hanging amid Victorian pieces of furniture. The tapestry will be almost as good as new, but some of the beads may be missing. They are quite easily replaced, a separate back-stitch being used to secure each bead, if you can match them sufficiently well.

To remove dirt, a gentle but thorough brushing with a clothes brush does wonders, and the tapestry portions may be cautiously rubbed with a rag dipped in petrol.

Tufting or Candlewicking

This lovely old embroidery has the appeal of great simplicity. That appeal, combined with the boldness of this type of embroidery and the ease and quickness with which it is worked, has rescued it from oblivion in recent years and given it a posthumous popularity. It was revived in the United States, its birth-place, some years ago, then became a home-worker's craft in Canada and so arrived over here in the form of handsome and vivid cotton bedspreads.

Candlewicking, its other name, gives an idea of its history. In bygone centuries when America was a British colony, candles were made at home from a special thick white cotton, known as wicking, imprisoned in a column of grease. Some clever housewife discovered that this immensely thick cotton thread could be used to run-stitch flowing designs on loosely woven materials. If the cotton was then cut through wherever it lay on the surface, and the material washed, the wicking would thicken up into knots or tufts which remained firmly embedded into the stuff.

As the work was coarse, but covered large areas quickly, it was found particularly suitable for bedspreads. Modern Canadian

FIG. 92. Canadian bedspread, tufted in white and green on a paler green cotton crêpe

tufted bedspreads are made in just this way, usually in white and one deep vivid colour on cotton crêpe of a paler shade (Fig. 92).

The thick candlewicking with its "digging in" properties is not obtainable on this side of the Atlantic, but after some experiment I evolved the dashing English variant shown in Fig. 93. This is worked on a loosely woven linen in plain-coloured or rainbow embroidery wool, used double.

Wool will not thicken up like candlewicking, so the running stitch is altered to make firm tufts which will not pull out. This tufting stitch, as I call it, is described on page 180. It is used to outline the whole design.

If you want a small portion of the pattern to stand out boldly (a flower centre, for instance) fill it entirely with tufts. Or when time does not press, you can fill in the whole design in the same way, working close rows or circles of tufts according to the shape to be filled. You will then get a pile effect, rather reminiscent of a carpet.

By using rainbow wool you can get great variety of shading without the bother of thinking it out. You just take the colours

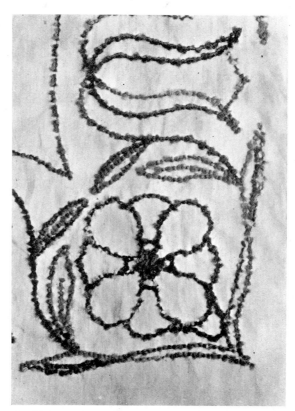

Fig. 93. This modern tufting is done in double-shaded wool on loosely woven linen, using the tufting-stitch described on page 180

as they come. When tufting anything finished with a hem, hold this down with one or two lines of tufting-stitch.

The work is effective for cushions, curtains and pram covers, as well as bedspreads.

SPIDER'S WEB WORK

This striking embroidery is not antique like samplers and tapestry, but it does belong to the past, though a more immediate one.

Occasionally one finds someone working it nowadays, and the specimen illustrated was made by a soldier during the Great War, when there was a short-lived vogue for embroidery as a man's hobby. But the palmy days of spider's web work were in the first few years of this century—half a life-time ago.

At that time a special soft canvas, checked alternately in white and a pastel colour, was sold for the work. A spider's web (sometimes called a wheel) was worked in a thick thread on either all the white or all the coloured squares, and gave a handsome result for night-dress cases, cushion covers and table-cloths.

A later development was to use glass-towelling, line-checked in inch squares, for the work, as in the illustration, and as the canvas is never seen nowadays, this must be your plan of campaign if you take up this really effective form of hand stitchery. As it is slow work making a web in each alternate square, in the 1900 style, it is worth trying the quicker plan shown in Fig. 94.

On this cloth a border of continuous spider's webs, black and golden-yellow alternately, is worked all round the edge. There is a similar inner oblong five squares farther inside, and at each corner the two lines are connected with a diagonal of four webs. All the other check lines are worked in chain-stitch, the colours being alternated both ways.

A variation more convenient for an afternoon table-cloth, as giving a smooth central surface for the china, is to leave blank all check lines inside the inner oblong, but in this case the working must be wholly or partly in thread matching the red or blue of the check lines.

Linen towelling makes pleasant runners if embroidered with a simple pattern of spider's webs at each end. It is also nice for chair-backs with the webs worked at one end only.

Curiously enough, while reading the proofs of this book a striking instance has occurred of the remarks made at the begin-

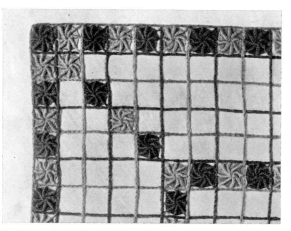

FIG. 94. Part of a table-cloth worked in spiders' webs on checked glass-towelling

ning of Chapter XV about the ebb and flow of popularity in any given type of embroidery.

When I wrote this section spider's web work was all but dead. Just recently, visiting Paris, I found it the newest craze there in a modernized form. Round flowers of daisy type occurring in simple outline embroideries are worked by the Frenchwoman as spider's webs or wheels in shaded thread—and very effective they are. Just try for yourself.

TUFTING AND SPIDER'S WEB STITCHES

For tufting, as described on page 176, use the following very simple stitch.

Tufting-stitch. Bring the needle through from the wrong side, and take running stitches about one-third of an inch long. Between every two running-stitches make a *short* back-stitch. Cut all the running-stitches through half-way between the back-stitches and you will have a series of puffy little tufts along your outline. The longer you make the running-stitches the more upstanding are the tufts and the greater the distances between them.

Spider's Web, or Wheel. For spider's web work (Fig. 94) the stitch—more properly, the pattern—is a simple combination of cross-stitch and overcasting.

First make the spokes of the wheel by making a large cross-stitch which fills a square on the glass-towelling, and working over this a plus sign, also filling the square. The two combined make an eight-spoked star or wheel. Now, starting from the centre of the wheel, where the spokes cross, overcast round and round outwards by taking a back-stitch over the spoke behind the needle and then passing the needle under that spoke and the next ahead of it. Back-stitch over the second spoke just gone under, then go under this and the next, and so on.

Continue round and round till the edges of the square are reached, as in Fig. 94. Or if a more open effect is wanted, work only half-way up the spokes. All overcasting stitches pass between the spokes and the material, not through the latter.

Chapter XVII

NATIONAL EMBROIDERIES

WHEN you have a love for embroidery, you will soon find that you become interested, not only in what you do yourself and what your ancestresses have done, but also in the hand stitchery of other parts of the world. Nowadays national boundaries are far less rigid than they were, since modern inventions such as the aeroplane and wireless have bound the whole world together with much stronger links.

Yet still almost every country has its typical embroideries. You will see them at national exhibitions, you will buy specimens of them when you cruise or travel abroad, and friends from distant parts will bring them home to you. Therefore, I think that you will be glad of some brief notes about the hand stitcheries of various countries and the qualities which they embody by means of needle and thread.

Various countries are given below in alphabetical order for easy reference. Where a well-known country is not mentioned, it is because, as far as I can find, it either has no typical needlecraft or produces fancy work which cannot be counted as embroidery. For instance, Germany does not seem in modern times to have any characteristic fancy-work form, while that of Belgium is perhaps hand-made lace, which is outside the scope of an embroidery book like this.

BULGARIA (and other Balkan countries, more or less). Bulgarian fancy work chiefly takes the form of dress embroideries for use on national costumes—especially sleeves. Borders and patterns are worked in closely set rows and panels on white washing or black materials. Bright colours—blue, green and a characteristic gay orange-red—are used, and are often outlined with or separated by lines of black. Cross, tapestry and back-stitches are much employed. Patterns embodying the Cross are greatly used.

182

The keynote of the work is *vividness*.

CHINA. Chinese embroideresses are infinitely patient and apparently also have extremely good, close sight, for much of their work is close and tiny in the extreme. Minute cross-stitch designs in clear, bright colours often decorate fine lawn or linen; larger floral sprays on household linens are worked in pastel shades and delicately outlined with a fine black back-stitch. Their appliqué, done on creamy grass-linen (Fig. 95), is a small and dainty blend of cut-work and appliqué. The vivid-coloured floral appliqués are first stiffened and then held down with very fine open buttonhole-stitch, some of the spaces often being cut away.

The keynote of Chinese embroideries is *delicacy*.

DENMARK has two old and traditional forms of fancy stitchery which are not much known outside her boundaries.

FIG. 95. A typical example of Chinese embroidery—delicate appliqué on grass linen

(1) The island of Amager, near Copenhagen, has given its name to a very charming shaded wool embroidery several centuries old. Clusters (especially wreaths) of the local flowers and shrubs provide both the simple but beautiful "full face" designs of massed flowers and leaves and the soft vegetable dyes for colouring the working threads. The work

has a Dutch character, from a colony from Holland which settled in Amager in 1516. The embroidery is done chiefly in satin-stitch, with minor touches in French knots and outline stitches, and used to adorn aprons, cushion covers and household linen.

(2) A 15th century white embroidery called Hedebo, which was worked on home-spun linen to adorn dress and household items by the dwellers on a heath (Hede) near Copenhagen. It was at its best about a century ago, when stitchery and designs were both exquisite. A modern Danish embroidery society has rescued it from oblivion in recent years. It is an elaborate and beautiful form of drawn-thread work combined with satin-stitched flowers and chain-stitched scrolls and looks like coarse lace.

The keynote of Danish embroidery is *sturdiness*.

EGYPT. The wandering tribes of the Egyptian desert make needlework pictures in hemmed appliqué, using various-coloured cotton appliqués on a thick creamy background. The scenes shown are always local ones, representing religious ceremonies or gods or the life of the makers—boys leading camels or donkeys, sphinxes, pyramids and palm trees. Small details are embroidered in simple stitches. The pictures are based on ancient Egyptian paintings and show the same curious perspective—or lack of it! This tent-work gained its name because its original purpose was to adorn the nomads' tents, but it is now made for export to Western countries as wall panels, chair-backs and cushion covers.

The keynote of the work is *symbolism*.

ENGLAND. Coming to the most typical embroidery form of our own country, it is difficult to decide between three—samplers, smocking and quilting. But smocking, though a traditional embroidery used for centuries to hold and adorn the gathers on farm-workers' smocks, is shared by the Hungarians; and the beautiful old quilting of Wales and the English mining districts migrated to America and took on new forms there. So on the whole we will plump for samplers, which in their motto and cross-stitch form seem to be entirely and wholly English. They are described in Chapter XVI and one is illustrated in Fig. 90.

The keynote of English embroidery is *simplicity*.

FRANCE, from a needlework point of view, is artistic only in streaks. Much of her fancy work is grotesque or definitely ugly, but for dress embroideries and certain simple house linen decora-

FIG. 96. French skill is shown in this dainty ivy appliqué, secured in place with a fine open-work stitch

tions (Fig. 96) she has no equal anywhere for grace and beauty of execution. Open-work stitchery such as *broderie anglaise*, punch-stitch and hem-stitching are perhaps her *chefs-d'oeuvre*, all of these requiring a lightness and nicety of touch which are typically national.

The keynote of French embroidery is *daintiness*.

HUNGARY. Though at such opposite ends of Europe, there is a strong similarity between the embroideries of Hungary and Scandinavia (Norway and Sweden) for both use needle-weaving and Hardanger work. Hungarian dress embroideries, usually on white voile or muslin, also mingle with these smocking (especially single cable and wave-stitches) and stylized floral motifs in heavy satin-stitch. The embroidery is lavish and very vivid in colouring, bright red, green, blue and black being used.

FIG. 97. Japanese embroideries use a bold satin-stitch and plenty of laid filling

The keynote of the work is *gaiety*.

ITALY might be called the queen of embroidery countries, so rich is she in characteristic types of fancy work. Cutwork is very specially Italian. So are the elaborate Italian hem-stitches, seldom found in the work of other nations, not to mention Assisi embroidery. These are all fully described in earlier chapters of this book.

Florentine work combines Italian hem-stitches and a little simple cut-work with typical stylized designs worked in satin-stitch and cord-stitch. These are formal in character, always ending in squared tendrils which give the work its alternative name of Tendril Embroidery.

The keynote of Italian embroideries is *formality*.

JAPAN's characteristic work is the very opposite of that of her neighbour, China. It is as dashing—not to say slap-dash!—as Chinese is painstaking, as sprawly as Chinese is compact. It is used for the decoration of kimonos (Fig. 97), truly Japanese flowers, such as the chrysanthemum and cherry, being lavishly embroidered on these garments.

The colours are gay and artistic, the matt cotton threads thick, to cover the ground quickly, and often ready shaded. Satin-stitch is chiefly used, even for stems. On large leaves it is worked right across as described on page 169 for laid filling, and then held down with lighter stroke stitches which are couched across it.

The keynote of Japanese embroidery is *effectiveness*.

NORWAY is well known for her Hardanger work, named after the equally famous Hardanger Fjord. This is a striking soft-canvas embroidery. Stylized floral or geometrical designs of simple character are counted out on the threads and worked in a mixture of satin-stitch (arranged in square or oblong blocks) and easy drawn-thread and cut-work stitches. The work is used chiefly to adorn household linens and combines boldness with delicacy.

The keynote of Norwegian embroidery is *dignity*.

PORTUGAL. From its colony, the island of Madeira in the Atlantic, comes the well-known Madeira work, made by the women as a spare-time industry to provide money for their dowries. This white embroidery is very like the French *broderie anglaise*, but it has no satin-stitching except of dots, which often link up the motifs. Old Madeira work was almost entirely eyelets, but modern specimens may have a few cut-work bars as well.

The work is an all-white embroidery, but sometimes, to save eye strain, the workers blue their threads before using them. The effect is not as pretty as the all-white, but the tint disappears at the first washing.

The keynote of Madeira embroidery is *grace*.

RUSSIA, as befits such a vast and varied country, produces several characteristic kinds of embroidery. All are of definitely peasant character, worked with very simple stitches in large, bold designs on some kind of linen. The designs are mostly geometrical or stylized, and are frequently filled with lines of close darning, as in Fig. 98. Cross-stitch also is sometimes seen or a rather coarse satin-stitch in colour, finely outlined with black back-stitch.

FIG. 98. This boldly darned linen curtain hails from Russia

The colours used are definite and well contrasted, but not gaudy as in most peasant embroideries.

The keynote of Russian work is *boldness*.

SPAIN. Embroidered shawls, beautifully worked in silks on a silken background, come to mind at once, for no cruise is complete without these shawls being offered from small boats to passengers leaning over the ship's side. The colours are often vivid ones on a black ground, but the most beautiful and typically national shawls, seldom offered to foreign tourists, are those in white with coloured embroidery or in black with entirely white stitchery.

Nowadays, however, Spanish shawls are so often copied cheaply, especially by the Japanese, that their wool embroidery is perhaps, more characteristic. Dashing floral stylized designs (or bull-fight scenes set in a floral border, as in Fig. 99) are worked in the most vivid shades of wool on a coarse, creamy cotton background, chiefly for cushion covers. The embroidery is mostly solid, a little satin-stitch being outweighed by a liberal use of Cretan-stitch (see page 97). The edges of the cover are worked over with blocks of satin-stitches, and the corners finished with variegated wool tassels.

FIG. 99. The Spanish bull in fighting mood! For detail of this wool embroidery, see Fig. 53

The keynote of Spanish embroidery, whether in silk or wool, is *vigour*.

SWEDEN is the chief exponent of the work variously called Swedish darning, Swedish weaving and needle-weaving, though it is also found to a less extent in Hungarian embroideries. The Hungarians, however, work it on fine dress materials, the Swedes on linens and crashes for household uses. This embroidery is fully described in Chapter XII.

The keynote of Swedish embroidery is *repetition*.

The United States has welcomed emigrants in large numbers from most parts of the world, and most of these have brought their own embroideries with them, with little or no alteration, to the New World. These still remain typical, not of the United States, but of their country of origin. Far more characteristic of America is her earlier needlecraft evolved out of the necessities of a life of hardship during the early Colonial days or freely adapted from embroideries brought over by the little ship *Mayflower*.

Tufting (see page 176), patchwork (though this is not embroidery) and the special American form of quilting, used between or round patchwork designs, are good examples. A more modern stitchery which seems to have originated in the United States during the last two generations is picture map embroidery (Fig. 85).

The keynote of American embroidery is *ingenuity*.

CHAPTER XVIII

TOUCHING UP AND ACCESSORIES

PERHAPS you have never heard of "touching up" embroidery? It is not surprising if you have not, for this is a term I have invented for adding mere touches of embroidery, in simple outline stitches, to accentuate and enhance the beauty of the pattern already on the material.

Touching up is an enthralling kind of fancy work for· the woman who likes something pretty and easy to occupy her hands, but does not want the bother of—or has not the leisure for—buying and stamping off a transfer or doing the whole of the work on a ready-prepared piece of material.

With touching up, the design is already there in the prettiest colours. You can put in just what amount of easy work you like, and for a minimum of trouble you will get a vivid, colourful wall panel, cushion cover, blotter or fire-screen.

Cretonne is the best—perhaps the only—material to use. Choose a design which makes a picture (like the garden sundial scene in Fig. 100) or one which shows flowers in a natural growing position. Then buy either cottons or embroidery wool in two or three of the main shades shown, choosing threads a little brighter or stronger in tint than the fabric colours, so that they will give extra life to the finished work.

You can choose for yourself whether you will put much or little embroidery on to your cretonne. In Fig. 100 only a light accentuation in outline-stitch round some of the main features, such as the sundial and the main flower outlines, is being attempted. The cretonne appliqué shown in Fig. 3, again, merely has petals outlined and leaves lightly veined in chain-stitch.

On the other hand, I have seen large cretonne pictures quite elaborately touched up, with all outlines worked, sometimes in spaced buttonhole-stitch, which is very effective, and sometimes

191

in split or stem-stitch. In addition, big areas were worked over with trellises of couching or sprinkled with French knots or seed-stitch.

The result was handsome and full of liveliness, I must admit.

FIG. 100. Cretonne in a picture design touched up here and there with outline embroidery

But there is perhaps a suggestion of gilding the lily in working so thoroughly over a design already complete in itself, and the amount of time taken is nearly as much as that required to embroider an ordinary design. I suppose that, really, touching up is almost entirely a matter of personal taste, and you must judge for yourself just how much to do.

It is partly a question of colour, too, for certain shades "pay for" being accentuated more than others. As you will see by Fig. 100, white is one of the most effective; so are bright pillar-box red, and jade and emerald greens. A touch of black gives effective contrast, but otherwise dark colours should be touched up only sparingly, if at all. Another use for this work is on something that has faded. Judicious touching up with threads as bright as, or brighter than, the original colours will often give a new and glowing look to the fabric ravaged by time or sunshine.

MAKING ACCESSORIES FOR EMBROIDERY

When you come to the making up of your embroidered items, you may find that they need little finishing touches which are not exactly stitchery, but are made with the working threads you have been using.

A gay tassel or two, a cord for pulling up a bag or a neckline or for edging a cushion—such accessories as these are often needed to complete the pretty effect of your embroidery. They look best if you make them yourself from the threads you have been using, for bought accessories cannot harmonize in the same way. They are very simple to fashion.

Cords are best made by plaiting. Regulate the number of thicknesses of the threads used according to the thickness of the cord wanted. A fine cord for fastening the neck of a voile blouse or child's frock may be made from stranded cotton, three complete lengths of six strands each being plaited together rather tightly. But for a thick cord to outline a cushion, three lengths of rug or eight-ply wool, used single, or of embroidery wool (four to six thicknesses in each length) will be needed.

The three lengths may be all the same colour, three tones of one colour to give a shaded effect, or all of different tints to achieve a rainbow result. You will find it interesting to try colour experiments with short lengths and oddments.

Remember that the plaiting shortens the strands considerably, so that they should be cut, say, one and a half times the finished length wanted. An exception to this is wool, which during plaiting usually stretches enough—sometimes more than enough—to counteract the amount lost. The tighter you plait, the more length will be taken up and the firmer the cord will be.

Tassels often make a pretty finish at the corners of cushion covers, work-bags and runners, and in addition they are needed to finish the loose ends of tie-cords.

To make a tassel, decide on the length it is to be, and cut a slip of cardboard that width and a few inches long. Wind the thread over and over this slip, width-ways, a dozen times or as many as are required for the thickness of tassel you want. Slip a short length of the same thread through the windings at one end and tie them together tightly. Then coax the half-made tassel off the card.

Give it a knob or head by binding it tightly with more thread a little below the first tying—say one-fourth or one-fifth of the distance down the tassel. Tie the binding cord and conceal its ends among the windings. Then cut the loops apart at the bottom of the tassel and even up the ends thus made.

Loops or slots may be wanted for running cords through, or for fastening, buttons. Work loops like buttonholed cut-work bars (see page 80) and slots just as for needle-woven bars (see page 122).

Chapter XIX

FINISHING YOUR EMBROIDERY

IF well begun is half-done, well finished is perhaps the other half of your work. Your embroidery is not completed when you put in the final careful stitch, for to look its best it needs painstaking "last touches" and just the right kind of pressing.

Also, after it has been used for a time, many a piece of fancy work requires laundering, and the life and beauty of your work afterwards depend on how this cleansing is done.

Do not think that these processes are very complicated ones. They are not. It is only that embroidered articles have their own little peculiarities, just like anything else you wash or press, and if you pay heed to these you will get the best possible results.

Finishing and Pressing

At the end of a piece of work, look it over carefully to see that you have not missed filling in any stitches anywhere. In a large or detailed job, it is easier to make this omission than perhaps you would imagine! When you finish any cut-work, before cutting away make sure that in every case the purl of the buttonholing lies against what will be a space, not away from it.

If you find any missing stitches or other small mistakes, it will not take long to put them right, and a much more efficient result will be obtained.

Next examine the wrong side. Any loose ends of working thread should be finished off securely; then cut away surplus ends which give an untidy look. These precautions are especially necessary on transparent material, as when doing shadow embroidery, for then any untidiness will show through to the right side. In appliqué or quilting, take out any tackings that are now unnecessary; in smocking, remove the gathering threads.

Pressing so greatly beautifies nearly all kinds of embroidery that it is well worth doing carefully. In addition to the ordinary ironing equipment of ironing board or table, spotless ironing-sheet, iron-stand, iron-holder, ironing slipper (if you use a flat iron) and press cloths, for embroidery a thick padding is needed under the sheet, especially for work or stitches that are much raised.

If pressed on a too lightly padded board, the raised parts will be flattened and much of their beauty lost; whereas they will sink into a thick, soft padding and keep their slight relief effect. You can use a piece of old blanket, doubled or folded in four, for padding, or my own favourite—one of those thick fluffy baby's cot blankets which are sold at the sixpenny stores.

Always press embroidery right side downwards on the board, so that the iron goes over the wrong side only. Most materials (organdie, some artificial silks and shantung are exceptions) require damp pressing. Cottons may be damped direct with a cheap sponge wrung out of (preferably) warm water; linens and silks respond better to a damp press cloth placed between them and the iron. Organdie, which requires relatively little heat, may have a dry press cloth or a double fold of tissue paper laid over it for protection.

Linen, in my experience, needs the hottest iron of all, as creases in it are easy to make and stubborn to take out without plenty of heat. Artificial silks and mixtures easily shrivel under what seems only a moderate iron and flannel (sometimes embroidered for babies' garments or as the under-layer in shadow quilting) scorches readily. So for these fabrics test the iron cautiously on an inconspicuous corner or hem.

Remember that pressing is not ironing. The iron must not glide but must descend and press firmly, being then lifted before it is put down again in another place. Press heavily on wrinkled or puckered portions of the fabric, which are generally between the embroidered parts, and more lightly on the actual embroidery.

After damp pressing, let the embroidery dry completely, spread out flat or hung carefully on an airer, before it is used or put away.

The foregoing are general instructions. Now for some special hints on the idiosyncrasies of particular types of embroidery.

Appliqué and Inlay. These are partly in a double thickness of material. The double parts may require rather liberal damping. Press both under and upper layer quite free of wrinkles and see that both layers dry thoroughly afterwards.

Quilting. For the English and pattern varieties, see the note on page 48. Press Italian quilting over a specially thick padding.

Broderie Anglaise and Cut-work. If these have puckered in the working, pin them out carefully on a board, damp them and let them remain so for several hours. Then transfer to a heavily padded ironing board and press well under a damp cloth. Button-holed portions will tend to hold the damp longest, so press these first, then the flat parts, and then the buttonholed portions a second time.

Wool embroideries look best if pressed only lightly, to preserve their elasticity and raised look.

Tapestry. If any puckering has occurred during working, damp the wrong side lightly, cover it with a dry press cloth of thin material and press very lightly with a hot iron. Repeat if required. Locker rug tapestry does not require pressing and is best without it.

Smocking needs a special technique. After finishing the embroidery and removing the gathering threads, pin out the smocking, right side downwards, on the ironing board, to just the required width. Cover it with a damp cloth, and pass an iron over it very lightly—rather just *touching* the folds than pressing or flattening them.

Tufting is usually worked on material, such as cotton crêpe or seersucker, which does not require ironing. Avoid pressing this embroidery.

LAUNDERING EMBROIDERY

Do not wash embroideries worked with metal threads. They should be professionally dry-cleaned. If you want to do them at home, however, lay them out flat and sprinkle them thickly with calcined magnesia. Roll up and leave undisturbed for two days, then shake or gently brush out the magnesia and it should bring the dirt with it, if the soiling was not severe. Try this for tapestry, too.

Nearly all other types of embroidery wash beautifully if they are carefully handled. Always wash these separately from ordinary things.

In the case of coloured work, unless you know that the threads used are guaranteed to stand great heat and the item is also very soiled, use a lather of pure soap flakes only moderately warm—not more than tepid with old embroideries on which the colours are not so likely to be fast. Very soiled white embroideries may be soaked first in tepid suds to loosen the dirt, but do not do this with coloured work. A preliminary soaking in *cold* salted water helps to set doubtful colours.

Wash quickly, squeezing and moving the embroidery up and down in the suds. Do not wring between the hands or rub, but use two or more lathers if the dirt does not vanish in the first one.

Rinse thoroughly in two just-warm waters. The wet work must not be rolled up, folded on itself or put aside for later attention. Carry the job through at once. Lay the piece flat between two folds of Turkish towel, and press out as much moisture as possible with your hands. If necessary, repeat with a second towel; the work should then be ready for the correct damp ironing. (Refer back, however, to page 196 where I give a list of materials which must be ironed dry.)

The hints already given for pressing apply also to ironing, except that now the iron glides instead of thumping. Carefully pull scalloped edges of cut-work or *broderie anglaise* into shape as you work. If the work has become too dry at any one spot, damp down by laying a damp cloth over it, not by sprinkling. When you want to avoid a shiny look even on the wrong side, as for items which may be seen on both sides, lay a thin dry press cloth over the work.

Generally speaking, shape is kept best, especially on round or oval items, if you iron outwards all ways from the centre.

Small fine items in thin material, such as handkerchiefs or modesty vests embroidered in *broderie anglaise* or drawn-thread, may be spread perfectly smoothly on a glass surface, such as a mirror or glass-topped dressing-table. Do this while they are wet and leave them until bone dry, when they should be as smooth as if ironed.

Quilting must be ironed lightly and you must not expect to get it as smooth as ordinary surfaces. Remember that if it is flattened out much most of its beauty is lost.

Remnants and Left-overs

I have called this chapter "Finishing Your Embroidery," and would like to end with a few remarks about finishing it *up*! The sad day comes when the embroidered item reaches old age and must be cast aside. Yet embroidery of many kinds is so durable that it often outlasts the material it originally adorned. When this happens, however small it may be, if it is in good condition think twice before you throw it away.

Of course, I am referring to work which is beautiful in itself and was carefully and slowly made. It is not worth while to keep simple outline fancy work, for instance, as this can be so quickly and cheaply replaced, but with a little ingenuity a beautiful flower spray or a well-worked pattern may often be put to some other decorative use.

This applies not only to embroidery you have made yourself, but to specimens of an earlier day. It is much more satisfactory to use these—carefully, of course—than to keep them folded away as museum pieces seldom or never seen.

Old samplers or other specimens which are fragile or irreplaceable often need the protection of glass and may be mounted either as pictures or as glass-topped trays or put under the glass tops of dressing-tables. I have seen a fine specimen of Victorian tapestry, a small circular shape worked long ago to cover a footstool, made into a delightful little round tray, so that it was safe and yet of daily use.

Less precious modern specimens have endless charming uses. It is easy to cut the actual stuff on which the embroidery is worked to a symmetrical shape, thus removing all worn parts, and mount this on a larger contrasting piece with the aid of a fancy stitch to cover the join. In this way quite small pieces may be utilized to lift a day or evening handbag into gracious distinction or to trim a garment.

An embroidered panel may do new duty as a scarf or be cut up to form "peasant" sleeves in a blouse. Tiny complete motifs often look wonderfully effective if made into "buckles" for belts, neck slots through which a tie is threaded or large decorative buttons. These are ways, too, in which you can use small foreign embroidery specimens bought on your travels or at exhibitions at home.

Again, a plain day dress may easily be "made" by the addition of a collar or modesty vest contrived from a fine bit of embroidery which has outlived its original use.

Have you, perhaps, some *broderie anglaise* left over, still good, from a worn-out item? It can be shaped into panels and let into a plain runner or a tray-cloth.

And for the bits and pieces that seem too tiny to be of any use at all, there is always the dainty fascination of "embroidery patchwork." For this collect not only minute bits of embroidery, but also scraps of fine lace, odd ribbon bows, fragments of rosebud trimming and so on. An artistic hodge-podge of these can be used to cover pretty boxes for gloves or dressing-table, made into the flap for a handkerchief sachet or arranged in an inexpensive little gilt frame to serve as a trinket tray.

The patchwork is easily fixed to its background with "Grip-Fix" or milliner's glue, baby insertion or ribbon being employed just as feather-stitching is used in crazy-work, to outline the various patches. Or do this with a suitable embroidery stitch.

And if the supply of embroidery for adorning a particular article runs short, it is the work of an hour only to use up oddments of left-over transfers and stray skeins of silk in working several small "remnants" to fill the gap.

INDEX

(*NOTE*. Where one entry has several page references, the main one giving working instructions is printed in BLACK TYPE.)

MADE IN GREAT BRITAIN AT THE PITMAN PRESS, BATH
C5 – (C.104)

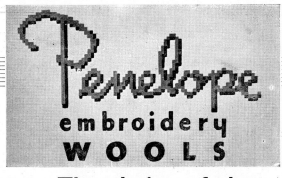

Penelope embroidery WOOLS

.... The choice of the experienced embroiderer

Penelope Wools appeal to your artistic sensibilities. It is a pleasure to work with them. Their subtle blending of tones and infinite range of shades make you master of every design you undertake. For ease in working and variety of colours Penelope Wools are the considered choice of experienced embroiderers.

Penelope CREWEL WOOL

PENELOPE CREWEL Wool is a fine worsted dyed specially to match the colourings of the original crewel wool embroideries of the sixteenth and seventeenth centuries. Use it for your Jacobean panels. (See the Penelope range of Jacobean Embroidery.)
Dyed in 25 ranges, 155 shades.

Penelope TAPESTRY WOOL

PENELOPE TAPESTRY Wool is extremely hard-wearing and therefore ideal for stool tops, chair seats or any other canvas work. We recommend this Wool for use on Penelope stencilled and hand-painted canvases. In the colour range you will find the correct shades for all period designs. Soft colours and rich colours; in fact, any colours you may require for an antique or modern scheme.
Dyed in 25 ranges, 155 shades.

Penelope ZEPHYR WOOL

This is the Wool for modern stitchery on linen or crash. Bright, cheery colours predominate in the range. PENELOPE ZEPHYR Embroidery Wool will wash and wear well. You can also use Penelope Zephyr on Penelope Canvas.
Dyed in 31 ranges, 156 shades.

M.S.E. EMBROIDERY WOOL

A new Wool for use on very coarse canvas. It is very thick and is recommended for quick and effective results. Most satisfactory when used on bold modern patterns.
Designs can be obtained stencilled on to special canvas for use with this attractive Wool.
70 shades.

PENELOPE'S SERVICE

Most good woolshops stock these wools, but if you have any difficulty in obtaining, write to me for the address of your nearest retailer.
I shall be delighted to help you with your needlework problems free of charge; a 1½d. stamp will be appreciated. Write to—

PENELOPE of
Wm. BRIGGS & CO. LTD., 34 EE Cannon St., Manchester, 4

W.B. Wools are GOOD wools

Hare W.B.70